The Fork in the Road Leads Home

Reflections from My Life's Journeys...
A Collection of Essays

By Fred Clausen

Invitation to Love

"The world needs and deserves the best version of each of us. We simply can't love others and all of God's creations if we do not first revere the beauty and love that exists in us and as us. It is by loving ourselves that we open our hearts and minds to the joy of living."

Fred Clausen

Dedication

The words and thoughts in this book are dedicated to my family and friends who have helped my life to become a wonderful blend of fun, love and adventure. I am deeply indebted to those who loved me, taught me, disciplined me, encouraged me and supported me along my journey. It is my sincere hope that these words will provide a looking glass into my life and thoughts for future generations of my family. It is also my hope that in some manner the words and thoughts within will make a meaningful difference for others as they seek to navigate the forks in the roads of their own lives.

Copyright © 2017 by Fred Clausen

This book is copyrighted material. All rights are reserved.
No part of this publication may be reproduced or distributed in any manner without prior written permission from the author and publisher.

IBSN# 978-0-692-98523-6

Published by
Fred Clausen, M.Ed., CAA
Irving Texas
469-556-2431

Cover created by Elyse Gappa

The Fork in the Road Leads Home
Reflections from My Life's Journeys…
A Collection of Essays

By Fred Clausen

Introduction:

At some critical moment in our life, we all stand at the proverbial *"fork in the road."* We take a long glaring look down each lane seeking to find the best route to our appointed destiny…to home. I've traveled the path of my chosen way to discover that it is the *"how"* of my journey that is significantly more important and impactful than the particular road chosen. I contend that although a choice inevitably must be made at each fork that diverges in our life's travels, the one we choose will be the right and perfect one if we are dedicated to playing the game by the standards that endorse and embrace peace, love, joy and understanding. I invite you to walk with me for a while as I seek to share and reflect upon my knowledge, insights and experiences from my life's adventures.

How much pure joy do you have in your life today? Does your life bring you joy? You know, that distinct overwhelming sense of happiness and pleasure. Personally, I awaken each morning, as many men do, to stare into a mirror, drag a razor across my face, brush my teeth and comb my graying hair in preparation for another day of embracing life. In my personal world, I rise to greet life with love and enthusiasm in my daily efforts not only to prosper, but to make a meaningful difference. I have lifted life's veil to find a maze of chaotic interactions and sublime experiences that I seek to learn from and share. I search to find the joy in every day, every experience and every person. The late, great Michael Jackson profoundly expressed one of life's greatest insights in his hit, "*Man in the Mirror.*" "*If you want to make the world a better place, take a look at yourself and make the change.*" The leader Mahatma Gandhi proclaimed, "*Be the change that you want to see in the world.*"

    The metaphorical icing on this philosophical cake that I share is derived from the famous poem "*Invictus*", by William Ernest Henley as he echoed the words, "*I am the master of my fate, I am the captain of my soul.*" "*Invictus*" is a powerful and moving term drawn from its Latin origins to represent the status of being *"undefeated"* or *"unconquered."* It represents a state of mind, heart and soul that illuminates our path to courage, self-awareness and enlightenment. It was the message of these lines, echoed day after day for over twenty years that sustained South African leader Nelson Mandela during his time of incarceration. The joyous, yet conflicting and laborious search for meaning and purpose in our lives must truly have its origins from within and then be manifested by our thoughts, words and deeds. Finding joy is our life's quest.

These essays are a personal collection and presentation of my thoughts, memories, ideas and experiences that have given me a more precise understanding of *"how you play the game"* --the game of life that leads to a richer, fuller and more meaningful existence. Each essay is an independent look at some of life's most important and challenging aspects. My time spent on the planet and my love affair with athletic competition stretched over sixty plus years, has introduced me to every sport related cliché known to man. It is both intriguing and amusing to realize how these sports inspired anecdotal quips often perfectly reflect some of life's greatest lessons. I will seek to blend in some of my athletic experiences as samples of the greater meaning for which I write. Life is exciting and unpredictable. It serves us up daily doses of challenges and opportunities and invites us to engage in robust participation, while luring us into a false sense of security. Just when we think we have mastered it, we haven't. Life promises us nothing, yet offers us everything that we can dream.

As I mentioned, the shared ideals that follow here have been gathered from my own journey. I am the only *"man in my mirror," "the master of my fate and the captain of my soul,"* just as you are in your life. I have engaged through study, prayer and meditation to become self-aware but not self-absorbed. My eyes have been opened to the rewards of having a servant's heart. I seek to find the joy in my life and to foster it as well. I share with you through these words the opportunity to gaze reflectively into the traits, beliefs and behaviors that make you unique and special. I challenge you to examine ways to make yourself and our world better for all of mankind.

In a future time and place as you sit on a beach, walk through the beautiful fall foliage or simply take pause to look back and ponder the purpose and meaning in this the ultimate game, it will be *"how"* you lived your life that will bring you peace, contentment and joy. I grade myself now by much different standards and with a much different curriculum than I did in my younger years. I have run my races for fame and fortune. My only goal is to measure what I have done in this life for the *"team."* By that, I mean my world and humanity. It is the impact of your deeds and actions on the peace, love and understanding in the world that will be remembered. Your legacy will be whatever you have chosen to paint with the canvass and brush that God has provided to you.

The axioms that I present in these pages were not learned easily nor perfected without the anticipated number of scars and growing pains. They were often ignored at their first revelation in my life as I sought to make my own way with my own plan and my own guidance. I discovered that this was not a very good strategy. Just as in athletic competition, our degree of success is often dependent on others. We are not in this game alone. There are dynamics within our thoughts and souls that out of necessity make life a team sport. It is our relationships that will prove to be the most critical element and vital to finding our way and reaching our ultimate joy and purpose in life.

We will look in a candid way at all the relationships that we need to create a meaningful life. A good starting point is what I like to refer to as my *"Sand Box Philosophy."* We learned as little children that sharing is caring. We romped joyously through those early years. We were taught the *Golden Rule* of treating others the way we want to be treated. We were accepting of others and unaware of differences until someone in our environment infected us with hate, doubt and fear. We saw our youthful innocence and joy dissolve into the confusion of judgment and separation. With a trusting heart we opened the door and unknowingly allowed our enthusiasm for life and creative energy to be sapped. How did we lose sight of those simple loving guidelines as we grew and became more engaged in our lives? More importantly, how do we regain that lost zeal for lovingly engaging the world?

How we interact and bond with our own thoughts, actions and intentions brings us into new and meaningful opportunities to create relationships with others in our life. Jesus implored each of us to *"Love Your Neighbor as Yourself."* The part of these divine instructions that is most often overlooked is the inference that we should offer others the same kind of love, kindness, guidance and forgiveness that we provide to ourselves. We must find and love ourselves first and then extend that love to the world. Our joy takes seed within and then grows for us to distribute to others. We are the architects of our own reality. We dream our own vivid dreams and ignite our own creative imaginations.

As the months and years of my life have slipped by, I have grown happier, more content and at peace with how my purpose has revealed itself. It has had its tough lessons and hard knocks. Most problems encountered were self-inflicted, but each has provided a learning and growth opportunity. I have been blessed by those souls who taught me, loved me, disciplined me, showed kindness and patience as the story of my life has unfolded. It has been the persistent and frequent reoccurrence of the underlying truths and principles that follow that have given me the direction and motivation to find and share my joy. They have helped to forge my physical, mental and spiritual maturation and laid the foundation for my relationships with myself, my family, my world and my God. It is my hope that by sharing them with you it may assist you throughout your quest in the same manner.

Fred Clausen

Table of Lessons

It's Not How You Start, But How You Finish that Matters	11
Get in the Game and Awaken Your Spirit	29
Sudden Change—Coming Out of the Fog	43
Don't Let the Whistle Scare You—You Can Do This	55
Solidify Your Goals—It's Hard to Hit a Moving Target	69
The 40 Second Clock is Ticking—Call the Play	77
Keep Your Head on a Swivel—Awareness is Critical	89
Without Honor, No One Wins—Integrity is Paramount	101
Your Greatest Trophy—The Prosperity of Life	111
Champions Are Created By Those Who Finish Second	121
The Clock of Life Has No Timeouts	131
Harness the Creative Power of Your Imagination	141
Condition Your Body to Improve Your Game and Your Life	151
To Err is Human—To Forgive Sets Us Free	161
Teammates in Life—I Am My Brother's Keeper	171
The Game's Not Over Until You Complete You Bucket List	183
Parting Poem—If I Could	191

Lesson One

It's Not How You Start, But How You Finish That Matters

> *"The start of anything is the beginning of an opportunity to travel the road, share the experience and enjoy the trip. The ultimate measure of the success of our journey lies in what we have accomplished along the way."*
>
> **Fred Clausen**

    The pale orange light from the Paris night seeped through the curtains of our hotel room as I sat on the floor with my laptop. I was careful to be quiet so that my wife would not awaken from her peaceful slumber. After all, it was 4:00 a.m. in Paris and 9:00 p.m. the previous day at Busch Stadium in St. Louis. The green glow from my screen highlighted the internet broadcast from ESPN.com of the sixth game in the 2011 World Series between the Texas Rangers and the St. Louis Cardinals. Hanging on every simulated pitch and delayed update of the game, I had watched as the Rangers had taken game six to the bottom of the ninth inning with a two-run lead with two outs and two strikes on the batter. The blog chatter on the right of my screen seemed as excited and optimistic as I was.

The Rangers were one strike, one potential pitch away from a world championship. I held my breath as I watched the screen. The simulated pitch drifted towards home plate on the green diamond screen. I waited for what seemed like an eternity for the results. Nothing changed. Finally, the blog on the side of the screen flashed the words, *"I can't believe what I have just seen!"* My heart raced knowing that the Rangers had finally climbed from the abyss of major league baseball to the top of the world. Then just as quickly, to my horror, two runs flashed up on the scoreboard portion of the screen indicating that the Cardinals, down to their last pitch, had tied the game.

In what proceeded to be my greatest witness to the reminder that *"It ain't over til it's over,"* as quoted by Yogi Berra, I painfully watched the screen as the Rangers would regain the lead again by two runs, only to lose it again in extra innings and to lose the game. The next day, with their energy and enthusiasm drained, the Rangers yielded game seven and the world championship to the Cardinals.

Life often is a reflection in many ways of my simulated game experience that night. Many lives have had a tough and laborious start and graduated into an even harder existence. We climb towards the mountain top, to see it vanish right before our eyes. I have heard friends, family and acquaintances over the years extol how they wish that they were twenty, thirty or even forty again. They boast of the things that they would do, the dreams that they would fulfill, the money that they would make. *"If-Only"* becomes a mantra of existence to those who seek to recover lost time, energy and opportunities from their past.

My personal experience is that life tends to shrink and expand according to your level of courage and determination, no matter what your age. Life is painful at times. Life is disappointing at times. But more often than not, life will give back to you in exponential measure the time, love and effort that you provide in making your world and the world of those around you, a more loving and peaceful place. Success lies in learning to deal with the low times and the pain of living while keeping an attitude of hope and a positive outlook for the future.

The one irrefutable thing is that you can't win unless you are in the game and in it to win. The game that I profess in this moment is not a game at all, but the day to day living of our lives. I'm sure that if the Texas Rangers could roll back the clock to that game six ninth inning, the players and coaches would have each had an idea of what they could have done differently to alter the outcome. It is in retrospect that many of us choose to live our lives. We dwell on the perceived issues of our youth. We ponder on opportunities lost along our journey and provide energy to the shadows of our past that sap vital energy for us to excel in our efforts today and in the future.

In life, as in sports, you must learn from your mistakes to grow and mature. No one lives an error-free life. No one calls the right play or pitch every time. But as life is reflective of sports, it is what you learn in the innings, quarters and previous games that bring you to the final moments of determination that will set the tone and the opportunity for you to realize the prize. It is how we use what we learn along our path in life to fine tune our knowledge, plan and performance that will determine how we finish.

Where did I start? That is a very good question and one that I can only remember as far back as being a five-year-old. Life begins and ends with us in a state of confinement. As a child, we are confined by our inability to care for ourselves, protect ourselves and provide for ourselves. We then age and enter a state of self-sufficient living only to age further and, if we are lucky enough to live that long, return to a state of confinement and dependency at the end of life.

I am quite sure that many things preceded my early memories, but my first verifiable experiences center directly upon what would now be considered child abuse, or at the very least, neglect on my parents' part. I share these observations in jest because times in the mid nineteen fifties were different. We were a much different and in some ways naïve society. Times were simpler, families were closer, and the village actually did lend a hand at most times to raise a child.

Having been born on November 11th, Armistice Day, which is now commonly celebrated as Veteran's Day, my age did not allow me to start public school the fall that I was to turn five. Most public schools' age requirements are based on your age as of September 1st of each academic year. Once you have started school however, the age factor gives way to what grade level you have successfully completed. To solve that issue and the age gap for me, my parents enrolled me in Greystone Christian Grade School in downtown Mobile, Alabama. Since Greystone was a private school, the age factor gave way to the need for tuition-paying students to keep the school afloat. I was accepted with open arms and my parent's personal check to begin my education in kindergarten and then eventually the first grade.

Each day my grandmother, who lived with us, would walk me to the corner of a major highway to put me safely on a city bus to ride alone for eight miles downtown to school. Really???? At five years old? Of course, when I reached the school bus stop, a teacher would meet the bus and get me off and across the street and into school. Then at the end of the day, the process was reversed--teacher to bus, bus to grandmother and grandmother walking me home.

I can't totally recall, but I feel certain other parents must have been *"neglecting"* their children in this same manner on this bus circuit. Who in their right mind in today's world would even consider putting their five-year-old child on a city bus to ride alone for a half hour? As I said, those times were different. The world was different. Evidently, I survived and even prospered from the experience of my two-year bus tour back and forth to Greystone Christian Grade School.

Having completed both kindergarten and the first grade, I was now eligible, regardless of my birthday, to enter the second grade of the public school about five blocks from our home. The start of my formal education, and my parent's strategy to get around the birthday guidelines, had put me on an early road to a formal education. I often now just smile and shake my head at the thought of putting a five-year-old on a city bus alone. In this day and time, it would truly be considered neglect, or at the least, poor parenting. Be that as it may, the plan for my education, the goal and the strategy had worked for my parents and me. It was where I was to start and the earliest of my memories.

We have so many preconceived notions about life and how it should be. We tend to live our lives in a self confining box called our *"comfort zone."* This early experience of blended independence on the city bus and a disciplined approach to school quickly gave me a boost out of any perceived comfort zone I may have had at five-years old. It also helped to set the stage for my future growth and approach to life in general by revealing to me that those who achieve and prosper in life are those who expand or leave that comfort zone and face life and its challenges with courage and determination.

In my life there have been several times when the goals that I held dear to me at that moment in time, came into focus only to fade away into a mist of disappointment. Each of these moments led me to a greater understanding of how persistence and patience play a huge role in our lives as we strive to realize our potential. What often seems like a stumbling block is often the key component that hones us for something even higher than our own dreams. When we are young, we tend to envision our lives as being perfectly orchestrated and aligned with our dreams and desires. Then one day, reality slaps us in the face and wakes us up to the school of hard knocks.

As trivial as it may seem, my first encounter with the harsh reality of failure was when at the ripe old age of ten years old, I tried out for little league and didn't make the cut. When every friend and neighborhood sandlot teammate was chosen for a team, I failed to draw the attention of even one coach who would place me on his team. I was as good as, or better than, many of those chosen and awarded with the holy grail of every young aspiring baseball player; a brand-new uniform and cap. What had I done, or more specifically, not done, that left me standing out in the cold that whole spring and summer of youth baseball?

I had at this early age let my confidence and slight cockiness get the best of me. I had a goal, but no concrete plan. I assumed that the world would throw itself at my feet in adoration if I just showed up. At every tryout, workout and audition for the teams that spring, I moved to a different position to exhibit my skills. I was going to show the world that I could do it all! Who would need a team when I could be a superstar at any and all positions? In the process of never showing up in the same place twice to demonstrate a consistent mastery of the ability to play that particular position, I was unable to attract the attention of those coaches searching for a solid position player to fill out their squad. My official baseball and athletic career had begun with a resounding thud! I was determined that it would not end that way. I came away in tears but with the knowledge that I needed a lot more humility and definitely a better game plan.

The next spring, after enduring watching all my friends play through a season, I once again summoned up the courage and put my fractured ego on the line in the tryout process. This time however, armed with the harsh experience of failure and a burning desire to succeed, I spent all four tryout sessions working as an outfielder. I took every opportunity to showcase my fielding and throwing abilities to the coaches as they scouted us. I also demonstrated that I could do well with the bat. This new strategy worked. I was chosen to be a player for the B&H Food Store Red Sox. What a day!

The most interesting side note is that I never spent one game as an outfielder that year or any year in youth baseball or high school. The coach needed a catcher, which to most ten-year olds does not seem like the glamour position for baseball. In our backyard leagues, where teams often consisted of four or five players on each team, no one even had a catcher. Someone's house usually served as our backstop and the pitcher was charged with covering home on any plays at the plate. To my young mind though, becoming a catcher seemed like the perfect fit. I learned quickly that I got to participate on every pitch in the game and had the opportunity to direct the pitcher and provide strategic input to both infielders and outfielders. I guess it was the early signs of the coach in me creeping to the forefront of my mind.

My little league career in Mobile, Alabama while starting slowly, quickly blossomed into one of my life's greatest experiences. As an eleven-year-old, I was selected to the South Brookley All-Star team as a back-up catcher. Though laden with talent, our team didn't advance very far that year. We did, however, lay a foundation of big things to come. The following summer in 1964 as a twelve-year-old, I was selected again to the South Brookley All-Star team, this time as the starting catcher.

The 1964 South Brookley All-Stars earned a place in Mobile folklore as we battled to earn the district championship, the area championship, the state of Alabama championship, the South Regional championship and finally a berth in the Little League World Series in Williamsport, Pennsylvania. In the span of only a few short years, I had gone from a man without a team to boarding a plane to travel to places in the world I only knew existed in my seventh-grade geography book.

That magical summer as a twelve-year-old, spent traveling the country playing baseball, laid the foundation for my love for athletics and the many lessons learned in years to come. Our trip to the World Series in 1964 yielded a third-place finish. I celebrated hitting a towering home run in the game that we lost to Monterrey, Mexico and were eliminated. I also got thrown out trying to steal second base to end the game. As any twelve-year-old will tell you, if you make the last out in a game, no matter what else has transpired, then you are the one who lost the game for the team. That was the burden I had to bare for a few hours; but then the resiliency of being twelve-years-old took me back to the joy of youth in a short time. We went on to beat Japan in the consolation game and finish third in the series that year. Not a bad finish out of four-thousand teams in the world at that time.

As we dried our tears of disappointment, the *"Bama Boys"* as we were known, quickly recovered to enjoy a trip to the 1964 World's Fair in New York. We were also treated to an afternoon at Shea Stadium to watch a Mets game and meet with the Hall of Fame manager Casey Stengel. What a summer. What an experience. What a magnificent opportunity I would have forfeited had I not chosen to overcome the initial disappointment and find a new plan and path to my goals. I learned early that persistence pays off. I learned that trying to do it all will sometimes result in you not being chosen to do anything. Most of all, I learned that there is no "I" in TEAM.

Life, like the tide that I grew up with on Mobile Bay, is an ebb and flow that neither ceases nor remains the same. Today's success will fade into the new challenges that tomorrow will provide. Finding your role and contributing to a team effort is a shared experience that can pave the road to success. This early lesson gave me a brief look and sample of the process that one must develop in life to deal successfully with the valleys and the mountain tops. You must show up and compete, even when it seems tough and the odds are against you.

As I grew, matured and aged, it was stamped into my mind that you truly are *"never beaten unless you quit."* I'm quite certain that my coaches told me and my teammates something similar in each sports experience that I ever had. If we will persevere in life and work hard to focus on our goals, we have a chance for success. If we offer our skills to blend with those of the rest of the team, we all stand a greater chance to win. If one dream dies, then have the courage to dream a new dream--a bigger and better dream. Hope is the extension of our vision, and hope is also one of our greatest motivators.

My initial little league esson eventually led me to a promising high school athletic career at Holmes High School in San Antonio, Texas. When the local Mobile, Alabama Air Force base, Brookley Field, closed in 1966, my mother, a civil service worker, and I moved to Texas. I fearfully and grudgingly left my childhood friends and teammates back in Alabama for a new chapter in my life. Just when we have proven ourselves to those around us, the venue changes and we start again. Isn't that what life is all about: proving ourselves repeatedly while adapting to change and adjusting our dreams? Nothing stays the same for long in life.

At age fourteen, I was dropped into this new melting pot of talented students and athletes to find my way. My parents had divorced, and my Dad remained behind in Alabama. My coaches became my male authority figures and role models. My baseball talent served me well as I was able to not only make the varsity squad at Holmes my sophomore year, I was the starting catcher. I also played football as an adequate defensive end on a team trying to drag itself out of what was at that time the longest losing streak in the state. The transition seemed to match my goals and dreams of eventually becoming a professional baseball player. Athletic participation in my new environment helped me to assimilate quickly.

My high school athletic career was fun and exciting. Our football team did turn it around and we had winning seasons both my junior and senior years. My baseball skills continued to improve, and I became a solid All-District performer both my sophomore and junior years and a San Antonio All-City choice my junior year. Heading into my senior season I was named a baseball team captain and appeared headed for a college scholarship or a shot at pro baseball at some level. Mistake number two in my young life was quickly catching up with me. If you relax and get comfortable and satisfied with where you are in life, most likely that's where you will stay.

As my senior year unfolded at Holmes, I had a great football season and headed into baseball with eager anticipation. I'm not sure what exactly changed for me that spring. Maybe I had gotten the *"big head"* from past success. Maybe pitchers started paying more attention to me and giving me less fastballs to hit. Most baseball experts will tell you that the difference between a good hitter and a great hitter is the ability to exercise patience at the plate and to hit the curve ball. I could do neither that spring. My batting average, which had hovered in the high 300s during my sophomore and junior years, now resided below the 200 mark. The only thing mounting quicker than my strikeout numbers was the degree of total frustration that I felt. I pressed hard to right the ship, but with little success.

All of the attention that I had garnered in the previous years had melted away. No college was interested in giving a scholarship to a high school player who was not even hitting his weight. Devastated and at a loss about how to handle the situation, I found myself one night in the school yard across the street from our house just staring up at the stars and crying one of those *"why me"* songs to God and the universe. I had come full circle from not making the little league team in 1962 to becoming a high school player with budding potential who now could not attract even one scholarship offer.

I did have one shinning and unforgettable moment that senior season. In my last time at bat in my high school career, I hit a grand slam home run to boost the team to a 5-4 victory over Seguin High School. At least I had that moment to hang on to. Sadly, it was also my last game to play for my role model and hero, Coach Nelson Bippert. This was a man of great character who taught me so much more than baseball. He taught me how to work hard through physical pain and mental stress. He taught me how to be sharing, loving and kind, yet firm in my values and discipline. He changed my life for the better and filled the gap left by my father's absence in those years. He stood by me that senior season and encouraged me to stand fast in my self-confidence and to not give up on myself or my dream.

As I had struggled through that season, it became depressingly apparent that a scholarship was not in my immediate future. My academic achievement grades were very good, so plan B kicked in and I applied and was accepted to the University of Texas at Austin. I was determined that I would walk on and try to make the baseball team of one of the top programs in the country. Once again in my life, persistence and fate as it were, intervened and my plans and direction changed overnight.

Each summer in San Antonio, there was an annual summer All-Star baseball game made up of the best high school and college athletes in the South Texas area. The teams were coached by some of the local college coaches, and the players were chosen from hundreds of candidates who went through multiple days of tryouts and scrimmages. I was determined to showcase my skills one last time to at least prove to myself that I hadn't lost my skills, only my confidence. For the second time in my athletic life, my determination not to give up paid off. During the series of tryouts and scrimmages, I had a great streak of hitting and exhibiting my defensive skills as a catcher--so much so that I was one of only twenty players, out of several hundred who tried out, chosen for the San Antonio All-Stars. More importantly, I also had attracted the attention of Coach Elmer Kosub, the head baseball coach at St. Mary's University.

During the All-Star game that year it was as if I could do no wrong. I played only three innings as the coaches strived to get all of the players into the game. I made the maximum use of my time by throwing out three base stealing threats to end the first three innings and then hitting a double in my only at bat. I received numerous votes for the Most Valuable Player award. However, more exciting than that, after the game, I received an offer from Coach Kosub for a partial baseball scholarship and some work-study opportunities to attend St. Mary's. I was back! Coach Kosub took a chance on me. He would also be instrumental in me being selected as a player on the United States Baseball team for the 1972 Latin American Friendship Games in Managua, Nicaragua. My first coaching job came at the tender age of nineteen upon his recommendation to the leadership at St. Anthony's High School. His fatherly care and inspiration provided the spark and support that I still treasure to this day.

So, there I landed at the tender age of seventeen having already had two distinct lessons in life through my athletic participation and the relationships with my two mentor coaches. My eyes were opened wide, but many new lessons awaited me. Life is painful at times. Life is disappointing at times. Success lies in learning to deal with the low times and the pain of living while keeping a positive outlook and attitude. You must persevere and stay in the game. You must be open to a change in your approach, your knowledge and your attitude. The only thing in life that is certain is that *"change"* is inevitable. There is no static state in life. You are either growing or dying and we make that determination daily. Some define *"insanity"* as the approach to life in which, as creatures of our habits, we continue to repeat the same nonproductive behaviors methodically while expecting a different outcome. There is little in life that is absolute or what we might call *"black and white."* We are usually stuck contemplating the middle ground.

The spring of 1971 brought a new and sobering experience to me. The man who had become like my older brother, my mentor, my friend, Coach Bippert died after a courageous battle with brain cancer. He was thirty-two years old and left behind a wonderful wife, two young children and a church full of young athletes whose lives he touched in such a short period of time. Here was a man whose life, although short, made a profound and meaningful difference in the lives of others. That is what I wanted. I had determined that this was the servant leader that I would pattern my life after moving forward. Coach Bippert's passing was my first true experience with the death of someone extremely close. It opened my eyes to the fragile nature of life and our need to never waste a moment of it. My oldest son bears the first name *"Nelson"* in his honor.

Coach Bippert and Coach Kosub both taught me *"how to play the game"* --and I don't mean baseball. They both showed me how life is complete and rewarding when you lose yourself in the love and service of others. They taught me to strive to make a difference while I worked to make a living. They motivated my heart, mind and soul to be better. The truth is that we are prone to spend most of our lives toiling at something that we have no passion for. We take the advice of others or watch as someone else chases their own dreams not knowing what our own are. We spend many years lost in the false notions that money, things and achievements will bring us happiness. We are often left to make a judgment call about the purpose and meaning of our lives that can have a profound and lasting effect on us and those around us. I received my lessons and blue print from these men on how to make a difference in someone else's life.

Our lives are divided into little flashes of light and energy called days--those precious moments that we spend from the time we awaken until the time we return to peaceful slumber. Why are some of these days in our lives more important, more memorable than others? If indeed all time is precious, why then do we remember and celebrate some moments more than others? The answer lies in what we do, who we do it with and what we accomplish or perhaps fail to accomplish. The starting point of our lives is quite simply a point in a speck of time in the universe in which we begin to grace this planet. The start of anything is the beginning of an opportunity to travel the road, share the experience and enjoy the trip. The ultimate measure of the success of our journey is what we have accomplished along the way.

The measure of our success is not illustrated in how we start in our life, but how we live it as we race through the minutes, hours and days towards its completion. The magnificent poem *"The Dash"*, by Linda Ellis, is a great reminder that it is what we accomplish while we are here in that time frame between the date of our birth and the hour of our passing, that is important. The precious legacy of our minutes, hours, days and years is the prime indicator of our dedication to life, living and our fellow man. It is the profound and lasting impact that we make towards moving the world to a better, kinder, more loving place that should fill *"The Dash"* in our existence. I was born on November 11, 1951 and I will continue in my quest of living life to its fullest and making a difference until the date, at the other end of my life, is etched in stone. How will you fill *"The Dash"* in your life? Even if you stumble out of the starting blocks, it's how you finish your race that will matter the most.

Lesson Two

Get in the Game and Awaken Your Spirit

> *"If we fail to gain a spiritual awareness and reverence for life and the creative energy of God and the universe, we will have fumbled the ball and have swung and missed the opportunity for a happy and meaningful life."*
>
> **Fred Clausen**

Since my comparative writings here are a self-professed cross-section between athletics and our daily lives, it should come as no surprise that I will visit the subject of *"spirit"* in two distinct yet different contexts. The term *"spirit"* has a host of possible meanings; it might refer to our soul; another possibility is emotional energy; how about ghosts or even a type of alcoholic beverage? I seek in this narrative to bring into focus the need for our soul's spirit to become intertwined with our emotional energy's spirit in order to bring us to our greatest potential for finding ourselves, our joy, our purpose, our passion and our success.

The common denominators surrounding my inner-soulful spirit and the energy in action spirit is that both originate from within our thoughts and both have the potential to bring a high level of emotional and transformative power into our lives. *"Have you got that spirit?"* Remember the pep rallies in your high school or college days where the cheerleaders sought to intensify the atmosphere and infuse anyone within ear shot with excitement, energy and motivation to carry the team to victory? The recipe for success lies in how we harness our will and thoughts and then bring them forward in manifested action to serve the team--or on a much grander scale, our fellow man and the world.

Do you also recall the feeling of mystery that has tugged at your emotions as you have sought to find your life's direction and purpose? Have you sought answers to the *"Who am I, why am I here?"* questions that our spiritual hunger brings to the surface of our consciousness? Of course you have. We all have. So, the double barreled meaning of awakening these two forms of spirit in my own life has been in seeking to find and ignite my spiritual foundation and then using that strength and emotional energy to become immersed in the ongoing 24/7 everyday adventure that I call life.

I am always drawn to the following quote from President Theodore Roosevelt that captures the essence of becoming fully engaged in our life and efforts. Roosevelt was unquestionably one of the most energetic and spirit-driven presidents in United States history. Politics aside, he was in tuned with life, with nature and with the potential of engaging oneself fully in life, even when the energy-effort demands were extreme, and the critics were many. Simply showing up is the first and most important requirement for success and for growth. The words that follow echo his prolific challenge to *"get in the game!"*

"It is not the critic who counts; not the man who points out how the strong man stumbles, or where the doer of deeds could have done them better. The credit belongs to the man who is actually in the arena, whose face is marred by dust and sweat and blood; who strives valiantly; who errs, who comes short again and again, because there is no effort without error or shortcoming; but who does actually strive to do the deeds; who knows great enthusiasm, the great devotions; who spends himself in a worthy cause; who at best knows in the end the triumph of high achievement, and who at worst, if he fails, at least fails while daring greatly, so that his place shall never be with those cold and timid souls who neither know victory nor defeat."

As Roosevelt's words profess, we must engage ourselves to search out and achieve our best. To sit on the sidelines of life is not a viable option. Within each of us lie the seeds of greatness. Just like the tiny seed of an apple has the potential to become a great tree, bearing fruit, providing nourishment, beauty, and shade, we too have the potential to become great; achieve great things, provide nourishment and beauty in our own way to the rest of the world. This dormant spiritual energy lies at the center of each of us, just as it does in the tiny apple seed. Our responsibility is to activate and perfect our gifts.

Much like a locust, a crab, or a snake that sheds its shell or skin, our physical bodies are simply a vessel that surrounds our soul until it is time to cast it off. Why is it that we tend to spend more time in our lives focused on the outward appearances of our shells than we do on the thoughts and emotions that fuel and define us? We are spiritual beings first, going through a physical experience in life. We must take a bold and active approach to life so that the spiritual self and our spiritual energy can serve us in harmony. This spiritual awakening can only happen if we choose to engage, gear up and *"get in the game."*

It is not my assumed mission to advise others as to what is right or wrong or to steer you into any particular direction, religion, method of worship or path of spiritual development. No matter what your race, religion, creed or spiritual beliefs, we all should search for and acknowledge the beauty and light within us and in others. When questioned by the Pharisees in Luke 17:21, Jesus responded that the Kingdom of Heaven resides within each of us. I deeply believe that we are all the children of a greater power and energy, which I personally prefer to think of and acknowledge as God. As the brotherhood of man, we share many more commonalities than differences. We are teammates in this game of life.

If we fail to gain a spiritual awareness and reverence for life and the creative energy of God and the universe, we will have fumbled the ball and have swung and missed the opportunity for a happy and meaningful life. My purpose in sharing these thoughts is to nudge and encourage you to find your own spiritual awakening. It matters not what name adorns your house of worship or what path you choose to walk in that quest to become one with the spiritual center of your life. The important thing is to seek and find your spiritual identity and embrace it. Uncover your own distinct and precious light and let it shine for the world to see. A more complete and fulfilling life of peace and love awaits us.

My hope is that each of you will find the motivation to search for and find your own special relationship with the universe and the creative force that I recognize as God. My simple purpose is to plant seeds and sow the hope that you will be curious and courageous enough to diligently pursue your own path…your own answers…your own destiny. I have my own race to run; my own set of essential elements of leading a spiritual life to master. Each of us has to find our own perfect place of spiritual peace and develop our own special and individual relationship with the God energy within ourselves and within the universe. What we yearn for and what brings joy to each of us is as unique as our DNA or our finger prints.

The race we run to awaken our spirit is a marathon, not a sprint. We experience periods of growth and development both physically, mentally and spiritually. We also go through times of expanded awareness--awareness of ourselves, of our world, of others. We aspire to move to a higher plain of living, giving, loving, and understanding. To grow, mature and blossom our spiritual muscles, we must make a conscious and consistent effort to nourish our body, mind and soul. First and foremost, we must create a plan and exhibit a commitment for expanding our knowledge and get started. Read, study, pray and meditate to gain knowledge and clarity. We cannot wish ourselves to success in life--we must take responsibility and action. A journey of a thousand miles begins with the first step.

I can promise this: If we are drifting along aimlessly in life, God and the universe will provide some event, some heart-stopping moment to grab our attention--a wakeup call to our soul to move us to action. Why not be proactive, create your own energy and create your own path in life. Choose your own defining moment and actions rather than a response to a life-changing stimulus. Life shrinks or expands according to our level of courage and engagement in the creative process. We co-create with God and the universe our own existence. The game plan for that is up to us.

True spiritual enlightenment is not about religion. Religion often is about a specific set of rules and rituals established by man to fit their philosophy and perception of God. Religion, specific to any particular group, reflects a study in the history of and stories about great people who have chosen spiritual enlightenment and have put the principles of love, kindness and compassion to work in their own lives. The Christians, the Jews, the Muslims, the Buddhists, the Hindus and others share the common core values of loving the omnipotent God and loving your neighbor as you do yourself. Does the pathway that we choose to travel to God consciousness mean more than the obtainment of spiritual growth and maturity itself? I choose to think not.

The comfort and predictability of most religions is the attraction and road map to spiritual living. However, it is our spiritual nature itself that brings us closer to God and a more reverent understanding of our life and purpose. Being religious is not the same as being spiritual. I caution you to be keenly aware of any person or groups who teach the exclusion or damnation of those who don't acknowledge their perception of God and their religious philosophy. The historical manipulation of the masses by some religious dogma is well documented, as men have for centuries bent the words of God to accommodate their own worldly agenda. When we search for an avenue or conduit for our own spiritual growth, it should be centered on peace, love and understanding.

The acts of exclusion, persecution and judgment do not reflect spiritual maturity. I am my brother's keeper in my own Christ consciousness. God expects me to care not only for myself, but also for those who, for whatever reason or circumstance, cannot help themselves. Find the spiritual pathway that allows you to breathe in the goodness of our world and those around us. Embrace spiritual growth and a philosophy that is anchored in seeking and enhancing the good and beauty in all of God's creatures and creations. For spiritual growth we must seek knowledge through study and interaction. We must spend time connecting with our spirit and universal consciousness.

Much like the coordination required by a champion gymnast on a balance beam, we must strive for a delicate balance and spiritual alignment in our lives. We can't live a life of spiritual and intellectual contradiction that puts our thoughts and actions at odds with the consciousness of God and the universe. We must ask ourselves if we can declare spiritual maturity without having an active compassion for our fellow man, for nature, for creatures of the planet and our environment. There is a universal soul and oneness that connects everything. We simply cannot embrace one aspect of the kingdom while trashing the others and call ourselves spiritually aligned.

Spiritual enlightenment is about following your own heart and mind and searching to discover the intrinsic good in yourself and others. If you study the world's great religions, they are all based on the greatness and goodness of God. The name for God may change and the historical spiritual messenger may vary, but the universal message is the same. We are all the perfect creation of a loving God and power in the universe. Let love, caring and compassion for your unique spirit and that of others guide your life and behavior. Develop and flex your spiritual muscles daily by practicing relevant study, prayer and meditation. Awaken each day and go into the world to make a difference and to be a blessing.

Follow the example and teachings of Jesus, Buddha, Mohammed and others enlightened by love and peace. Focus on what these master teachers taught and how they lived their daily lives among the most common of people. None of these great spiritual teachers had the intent to start a religion. The core of their works, teachings and existence was to show us the way to live a daily life of love, peace and service. They exemplified a life of spiritual awareness and enlightenment. Don't allow the religions about these teachers that came from later interpretations and dogmas created by others, cloud your spiritual vision.

We simply cannot live our lives in a spiritual void and expect to have a happy and productive existence. Our perceived *"COMFORT ZONE"* can often become extremely uncomfortable when it mutes and stunts our physical, mental and spiritual growth. Nothing stays the same in life. The days and years come and go. The seasons change. Like every other living thing in nature, we are either growing or dying both physically and spiritually. Our task is to feed our hunger for a more perfect spiritual life. We must search, find, realize and exhibit the love and goodness within ourselves. There is a sports related cliché that states, *"You miss 100% of the shots that you never take."* Engage in spiritual training--take and make the shot.

Life experience has taught me that if your spiritual being is not acknowledged and nurtured, your life will never be full, happy and complete. What is inside of us determines our outward actions and reactions to the world. We are the creators of our own reality in life. Realizing and embracing the Christ-like things in our lives will bring more of Christ's blessings to us. We are not here on earth to spend our time and life awaiting the rewards of a coming kingdom in the clouds. We are here to be players in the here and now--to be in the game. We are here to co-create a kingdom of joy on earth; right here and right now that is aligned with God's peace and love.

I recall one lovely clear night in Destin, Florida when the moonlight on the Gulf waters seemed to form a lighted pathway to eternity. As I gazed into the moonlit water and waves, I saw a silver walkway into the distant dark horizon. The path could lead us anywhere we choose. It all depends on our spiritual and mental imagination. God is not into *"micro-managing"* the world. Things happen, situations occur and most often we have created our own world and situations through our thoughts, words, choices and actions. Life is as much about what happens within you; your thoughts, your spirit, your soul, as it is what happens outside of you. Your past is your *"experience,"* your present is your *"action,"* and your future is your *"potential."*

Realize that as you move through your life nothing has meaning or value until you share it. You only have a small window in life to share your love, wealth, knowledge, skills and to accomplish certain things. Don't miss the opportunity to share yourself, your talent, your love. There is a divine and natural flow of goodness and blessings in the universe. Joy in our life does not usually come in one large dose or blessing, but rather in small daily doses. Life is a team sport and it is played day to day. The more we embrace loving relationships and our connection to God, the higher the probability that we will create an enjoyable and meaningful existence.

That simple concept of sharing that we are taught in pre-school rings eternally true. Share your love, your time, your feelings, your dreams, and your support. Isn't that what we truly long for in our relationships with others? Isn't that what our soul yearns for in an effort to thrive and prosper? Life is a team sport. It is not our mission to carry the entire load for others. Every team member must man their own position; fill their gap; pursue the elusive ball. It should, however, be part of our quest to teach, encourage and celebrate the people in our lives and their accomplishments, as well as our own.

Spirituality is exhibited by living a life of service and gratitude. Take nothing for granted. Spiritual enlightenment takes time and work. It is a daily practice that requires the same attention to detail and discipline as the most gifted athletic skills. As part of our daily spiritual workout, it is important to bathe ourselves in an attitude of thanksgiving. Gratitude is a magical and magnetic force that tends to attract more and greater blessings into our world. We all like to hear the magic words *"thank you"* or *"I appreciate you"* ...so does God. The simplest, most personal and strongest of prayers is *"Thank You God."*

Each day is another opportunity to get better. We awaken from our nightly slumber to the present, renewed and leaving yesterday and the past behind having learned from the experiences. We welcome our new day of the *"present."* We are the creators of our own reality. Our thoughts are the seeds of creation for all our actions, and our actions produce our world. We visualize the world that we want to create. We must confront our fears and counter with a large dose of love. The truth is that fear is only an illusion of our subconscious self. All our actions or choices originate from either devoted love or perceived fear. These are the two ends of our conscious spectrum. It is our gift of unconditional love that creates unlimited potential in our lives and overcomes our fears.

It is our spiritual maturity and nature that gives us the understanding and undeniable fact that love is the center of living a happy and rewarding life. I am one with God and God is love. Therefore, I should exude love in every aspect of my life. Love will appear in our lives in many forms. It will come and go. It may be brief or lifelong. Whether it is fleeting or everlasting makes it no less love and noble in its pure state. There is much more to life than what we can see with the naked eye. The dynamics that fuel us reside in our hearts, our minds, and our knowledge. We must then educate our minds, our hearts and our souls to be loving, accepting and compassionate to ourselves and to others. Fear, anger and hate cannot survive in the presence of pure unconditional love.

Too often we procrastinate in life over things of the heart, not knowing if tomorrow will provide us with another chance to partake and enjoy. To love and be loved in all its forms, is one of life's greatest gifts. A life without love is a life that is incomplete and without meaning. Love yourself, love your partner, love your family, and love your friends--but LOVE. It is through love that we find our meaning and purpose in life. Enlarge your circle of love. Embrace those who are different from you and seek more understanding and common ground. Allow yourself to get close enough to see the love and goodness in others. Don't judge others on the superficial until you know what is in their heart and hear what is in their consciousness.

Living a spiritually rewarding and productive life is a *"hands on"* experience. When I took my young sons to my Mom's home I always made them go straight through the house steering clear of her delicate knick knacks, crystal vases and pictures. I would threaten them with, *"Don't touch anything…don't break anything…don't even look at anything."* When they came to stay alone with their Nan Naw, she carefully sat them down, talked about each knick knack, where it came from and what the importance was to her. They were things, but with lessons to be learned from each about some of life's most heartfelt moments. The lesson to me was that we can't simply tip toe through life without *"touching things"* and establishing relationships with others and still expect to live a rewarding existence.

The biggest challenge in life is to get off the bench and truly engage in living our lives to the fullest. Step outside of the constraints of your personal box and shift your paradigm and your awareness. You can never develop your potential in any area unless you are willing to put yourself into the heat of the battle and do the work. You must be willing to pay the price--to fall down yet get up and try again and again. The quest for our spiritual enlightenment and our peace and oneness with God is an exercise in planning, participation and persistence. The coveted prize is the joy, peace, love and contentment of having our soul find its true and perfect meaning in this life and beyond. All of our lives have a purpose. We are where we are supposed to be at the right and perfect moment in time. It is up to us to discover our purpose and fulfill our destiny.

Lesson Three

Sudden Change- Coming Out of the Fog

> *"It is through a change in our mindset, habits and actions that our lives gain more meaningful improvements and opportunities. Change is natural. Change is necessary, and change is inevitable."*
>
> **Fred Clausen**

On a cool and humid Friday evening in early October of 1978, I stood on the sideline as the defensive coordinator for the Crosby, Texas High School Cougar football team. It was the fourth game of a season that showed great promise. We had won two of our first four games against stiff competition and stood on the cusp of having a breakout season unlike any the sleepy Texas town just northeast of Houston had experienced in quite some time. Across the field our opponent, the Jasper Bulldogs, had taken early control of the game with a methodical powerful offense that had us reeling and on the ropes.

The stadium at Crosby lay in a low river bottom area only a mile or two east of the San Jacinto River as it wound its way down to Galveston Bay and eventually into the Gulf of Mexico. As the game wore through the first half, a misty blanket of thick fog began to roll into the stadium from the marsh land just to our west. It wasn't enough that we had fallen behind, now we had the issue of a rapidly deteriorating visibility factor to deal with as well. In sports as in life, we are taught to preserve and to deal with the elements as they present themselves. As this rugged game wore on and the fog rolled in, change hung thick in the air that fall evening.

Midway through the third quarter the Bulldogs mounted a drive that had them approaching our twenty-yard line. They were moving dangerously closer to a go-ahead touchdown that would put us in a hole from which we would most likely not recover. The fog grew so thick that our vision in any direction was becoming difficult to maintain and a clear view of the other sideline and even our own players was fading quickly. I frantically signaled in the next defensive call in hopes that the instructions could be identified by my captain in the huddle. To this day I am not sure that my signals ever reached his line of vision through the soupy mess in the air.

As the ball was snapped, the Jasper quarterback rolled to his left away from our sideline. The action and flow moved deeper into the fog as all twenty-two players and the officials became invisible. You might say we were playing blind, as even the opposite sideline and stands were now hidden from view. At last glance, the quarterback was seen launching a pass into the foggy night to where and whom it was unknown. After what seemed like an eternity with no visible confirmation and to my grand surprise, my defensive back emerged alone from the mist with the ball tucked neatly under his arm and headed in the direction of our goal line.

"Sudden Change" had manifested itself out of the wet cloud hanging over the field. From nothing in sight and no vision of the proceedings, we had turned the game around as my player raced ninety-five yards with an interception for what would prove to be the winning touchdown that night. I never saw the play, nor did anyone on our sideline. It was not even visible on game film footage taken from an elevated perch on our press box. All that mattered was that out of the fog of uncertainty that evening we had taken action and changed the complexion not only of that game, but of our entire season. We used a *"Sudden Change"* to alter the direction of our destiny. Our Cougar team would not lose again until the state Quarterfinal game in December.

Just like that evening in 1978, the *"Sudden Changes"* in our lives may come to us out of a state of mental, physical or spiritual fog, or in a moment in time that we least expect. It is how we adjust to these changes, be they good or bad, which can direct the flow and course of our lives. Change is often a wakeup call from God and the universe and a catalyst and opportunity for growth and adjustment in our lives…a chance to alter the direction of our human existence. If you don't seek to initiate change in your life situations at times, stagnation will set in. Success often comes from the way we seize the moments during changing situations and circumstances in our lives and take the ball in a different direction to score and alter the perceived outcome.

I have discovered on my life's journey that there are some very distinctive aspects to becoming happy, content and at peace with myself and the world. From the day we enter this somewhat chaotic world until the day we make our final exit, our lives are immersed in a process that is in a continuous state of revelation and wonder. Our lives are a parade of change and opportunity. The prime indicators for my perceived personal success lie in building a life of peace and contentment for both me and my family; for creating and sharing a life of prosperity; and for using my life talents and treasure to make a difference in the world.

As I continued to coach football for over twenty-four years in various Texas high schools, I became keenly aware of the dynamic effect of *"Sudden Change"*. In the heat of battle, one's ability to adapt to that change, more times than not, determines the final outcome. A fumble; a penalty; an interception; a big unexpected play that causes the nerves, muscles and emotions to amp up--that is *"Sudden Change."* *"Sudden Change"* in our daily lives can shift the momentum, swing the emotions, and shake your confidence level as well. It can render you helpless at any given moment to adjust your physical and mental mindset and to maintain the focus necessary to succeed. Change can be a catalyst or a road block, depending on how we embrace the concept and reality of that change.

How life unfolds for us is a universal combination of heredity, environment, education, effort, perseverance and a healthy dose of luck. Have you ever heard the saying, *"I'd rather be lucky than good?"* What if you could be both? The thoughts we have, the decisions that we make, and the actions that we take, set the stage upon which our lives will play out. Many believe, as do I, that through our action we generate our own luck. We are the lone architect of our past, present and future through our thoughts and actions. Change is inevitable, and we must develop the skills to deal with and prosper from those sometimes anxious and foggy moments.

Our success in life depends greatly on how we face our challenges, those *"Sudden Changes,"* and even the not-so-sudden ones. Do you look on problematic changes as a source of discouragement and a diversion from your goal? Or do you tackle change and challenges as an adventure that will provide more growth, strength and life experience? Problem solvers tend to be successful people. Meeting the challenges and changes in our life with the determination to find a way or a solution is what separates those who succeed from those who simply exist. We all need to learn and teach the skills of problem solving and embrace the opportunistic gift of change.

Every great invention, every great work of art, every great social shift in the world has originated as a thought in a creative mind with the intent to solve a problem or to open the doors and windows of our minds and souls. Creative minds foster change. A mind expanded can never return to its original condition. A soul provided with a deeper, richer and more universal understanding has unlimited power to both create and overcome *"Sudden Change."* So how do we cope with this *"Sudden Change"* in our lives, or any change at all? Our human nature is to stay in a state of comfort and familiarity. We often shrink at the thought and opportunity to venture out into the unknown world of change. We embrace what we know, often times even when what we know does not serve us well or advance us towards reaching our goals and achieving our dreams.

I have often in my career taken a new coaching job or athletic director's position because those who sought and hired me were not happy with the current state of their programs. They hired me to come in and be an agent of change. In athletics, in schools, in companies and other organizations stagnation occurs and growth is stifled when those in charge are no longer in pursuit of changes that can make things better. More than once my efforts, ideas and actions to provide positive leadership and change to a program, team or school district have been met initially with the phrase, *"Well we've always done it this way here!"* The actual meaning of this declaration is, *"We are comfortable and familiar with what is in place and what we know. Please don't take us out of our comfort zone, even if it is for the better."*

I have always been quite puzzled by that fractured mentality, especially because *"what has always been done"* had produced non-satisfactory results. Things weren't working. The results were poor, but we'll just insanely keep doing the same thing and expect a different outcome. In essence, the same people who hired me to initiate change had to first be dragged out of their comfort zone to become a part of helping it to happen. Change is not easy. It takes more energy for the brain to process new things. That is why change can be tiring, frustrating, and at times overwhelming to us. We tend to resist change because we are painfully aware that it will take more time, energy and effort initially, than just doing the status quo. The world revolves around change. Scientific laws tell us that physical matter is neither created nor destroyed--only CHANGED in form. Energy is neither created nor destroyed--only CHANGED in form. Change is natural. Change is necessary, and change is inevitable.

Our world, our life, our reality is in constant transformation. We live, we grow, we experience, we learn, we evolve or transform. Small changes help us to make better choices and move to a higher state of awareness of ourselves, our world and others. There is very little that is *"absolute"* in life. The only certainty is that change will occur. It is in finding how to negotiate and survive in the seasons of change that will determine our success. Just as no two snowflakes are the same, no two days of our lives are the same. Each day is a new opportunity from God, granted to us to change our life and world for the better.

Just think back ten or fifteen years and picture the world then as compared to the present. The technological advances alone are beyond most imaginations at that time. But thankfully, someone had the audacity to think outside of the box, dream big and take action. It is up to us through the gift of free will that we can choose to create a masterpiece with our life. The challenge each day is to show up and stay in the game. Our ego mind will tell us that life is too hard, the quest is too great; you'll never reach the goal. The world and even the voices in our ears each day form barriers to our success. It is the strength and wisdom to initiate change that wins the day.

The movie *Groundhog Day* is a funny and quirky illustration of how repeating the same actions and routine day after day can leave us in a virtual merry-go-round of life. Character Phil Connors, played by actor Bill Murray in the movie, finds his life in a time loop. An endless repetition of the same daily interactions drives him to attempt many ways out of the dilemma without success. It is only when Phil examines his life and changes his priorities that his life can find true meaning and move forward again. How many of us experience *Groundhog Day* in our own lives? We only learn and experience new things when we experience change. It is through change that we discover new insights about different aspects of our life. Each of us has things in our lives we would like to improve; finances, job, partner, friends, and many more. Even though we consciously know that nothing will improve by itself, we struggle in a spiraling death match with ourselves to resist meaningful change.

We all know that change is hard. Change is hard because our brain is hard wired to do the same thing over and over, regardless if that activity is good or bad for us. An athlete works hard to improve strength, speed, endurance and sport related skills. They are keenly aware that the body must change and grow to meet the ever-changing dynamics of competition. It is through a change in our mindset, habits and actions that our lives gain more meaningful improvements and opportunties. We never know what opportunities that change will bring into our world. By building a mental toughness that embraces and responds to sudden changes in our life, jobs, relationships and other areas, we are armed with more essential life skills. We become open to the infinite possibilities and prosperity in the universe.

Change triggers growth. Without a doubt, change pushes us into becoming more flexible and adaptable. By opening ourselves up to change, we are provided with a mirror into our personality that allows us to identify and improve the strengths and weaknesses of our character. We are able to expand our thresholds for accepting the possibilities of new and different ideas, experiences and relationships. We become a little bit more bold and accepting through embracing change. More often than not, changes encourage each of us to re-examine our life values and to look at things from a different perspective. The term *"open-minded"* means that we are willing to look at a variety of ideas and opportunities that can possibly make our world, as well as our own lives, better--more meaningful--more productive.

We must all become agents for change and seek ways to initiate *"Sudden Change"* moments in our daily lives that can be beneficial. My background as a science teacher taught me a series of sequential steps to identify problems and then devise a solution or plan for change. I have used the same *"scientific method"* steps in my coaching, my administrative work, and in my personal life. In lay terms, these steps include first identifying the problem or need for change. Then we must research the history, background and impact of the problem. From the research and gathering of data and knowledge, we then form a hypothesis or possible solution. The next step is to take that hypothesis and test it to see if indeed it will provide a viable solution. Once tested, we form a conclusion that then allows us to institute the needed change or to refine, adjust or start again from scratch.

In 2002 the General Manager of the Oakland Athletics baseball team, Billy Beane, had a chance meeting with a young Yale economics graduate named Peter Brand. The story is depicted in the movie *Moneyball* released in 2011 with star Brad Pitt playing the role of Beane. The premise of the movie is how these two turned the entire major league baseball world on its ear when Brand convinces Bean to use his new *"sabermetrics"* model to scout and sign players. *"Sabermetrics"* is the empirical analysis of baseball statistics that measure a player's in-game activities. The change to this method of looking at the potential of player's productivity allowed the Oakland team to become an instant contender on the league's lowest budget and payroll. The established MLB executives and coaches poked fun at and maligned the system at its onset. Today every major league baseball team uses the *"sabermetrics"* model as the core of their scouting programs. Life doesn't improve by chance. Our lives are improved through the thoughts, actions and courage of those who foster meaningful change.

It only takes one courageous person, one dreamer to light the fires of change. Christopher Columbus changed the world by sailing into the unknown to prove the earth was round. Martin Luther King, Nelson Mandela and Mahatma Gandhi changed the hearts and minds of the world about equality and human rights. Bill Gates and Mark Zuckerberg changed the world of technology and social media. Change takes courage. The secret to effective change is to center your thoughts and actions on building a new vision, not on expending energy to defend the old and status quo. When evaluating any challenge or situation, always ask the question, *"How can I change this and make it better?"* Change is both the growth and expansion of your knowledge, impact and influence. To resist meaningful change is to impede your own growth.

In athletics, coaches are constantly searching for *"impact players."* These are the players that through their attitudes, leadership, action and performance, can change the dynamics of any given game. In our quest for a more complete and meaningful existence, we must fight through the fog and roadblocks that often obscure our path. We must become *"impact players"* and agents of creating *"Sudden Change"* if change is the dynamic that will improve our lives and our world. World renowned leadership trainer and author John C. Maxwell sums it up wonderfully in his quote, *"As a leader, the first person that I need to lead is me. The first person I have to change is me. We cannot become what we need by remaining what we are!"*

Lesson Four

Don't Let the Whistle Scare You- You Can Do This

> *"Overcoming our fears presents us with the opportunity to open the door to a new awareness of peace, love and happiness in the world. Fear is a powerful emotion, but it only manifests itself if we give it energy."*
>
> ***Fred Clausen***

In 1973 after my graduation from St. Mary's University, I became the head baseball coach and assistant football coach at Cotulla High School in Cotulla, Texas. I was fresh out of college and raring to make my mark in the world. A note of trivia for future generations is that it was my first teaching and coaching position in the Texas public school system. I share the distinction of opening my career in public education in Cotulla with former President Lyndon Johnson. His first teaching position in a public school was in Cotulla as well. Of course, he was there about fifty years prior to my arrival to lay the groundwork and then moved on to slightly bigger things a little later. It is said that President

Johnson formed many of his perceptions on the need for equality and social justice while serving to educate the children of this small impoverished south Texas community.

Cotulla is the jumping-off place to cattle and deer country about half way between San Antonio and Laredo, Texas. The population swells each fall when deer season opens as hunters from all over the country flock in to bag the big trophy animals that run the brush and cactus-laden countryside. The inhabitants of Cotulla in 1973 were a cultural blend of the elite white ranch owners served by a few mixed businesses and workers from the overwhelming majority of Hispanic family households having deep roots to nearby Mexico. To say the least, most of the town's population of around two thousand was just a bit below what you might call *"dirt poor"* and with only a mild mastery of the English language. It was for the most part a collection of simple, good and caring people whose only desire was to have a safe and comfortable life.

The close proximity to Mexico also made Cotulla a center for migrant workers who spent summers in Minnesota picking sugar beets. With families crammed into one truck or station wagon, the workers would make the pilgrimage north and then return in the fall and work any small jobs available and to await the next *"migration"* back to the fields. Many of these migrant workers traveled and worked as entire families to maximize the sparse income that they could generate in a compacted harvest season up north. Through a Federal program initiated by President Johnson's administrative era,

Cotulla provided a special school to help accommodate those children of migrant families. They often arrived back to Cotulla in mid to late September after the end of the beet harvest and other seasonal work around the country.

I give you this background to set the scene for my simple, yet pointed illustration about how fear can grab control of our emotions and render our greatest skills and assets virtually useless. Fear is the root of many psychological issues in our lives that, when left unchecked, can manifest as stress, disease and a reduced ability to live a happy and productive existence. Nelson Mandela once stated, *"I learned that courage is not the absence of fear, but triumph over it. The brave man is not he who does not feel afraid, but he who conquers that fear."* We fear most the things that we don't understand or the things that we have been taught are a danger to us in some manner. President Franklin D. Roosevelt, in urging the country to remain brave and committed stated in the early days of World War II that, *"We have nothing to fear but fear itself."*

Throughout the centuries fear has been used as both a tool for motivation and a weapon for controlling the minds and hearts of impressionable people. Fear begins in our minds as a thought or reaction to some worldly experience and can quickly engulf our entire being leaving us helpless. Learning to recognize, manage and overcome our fears is one of our greatest challenges in life.

That brings me back to football season in Cotulla, Texas in 1973. As practices began we were short on numbers since most of the migrant population was just beginning to return from the beet fields. Each year another ten to twenty migrant students would help fill out the football team's roster. The coaches scrambled around and worked over time to help them catch up from missing the first couple of weeks of fall practices. Many of the players who showed up that fall were small in stature as is the general genetics of the Hispanic population. However, that year, among the migrant recruits loomed an impressive and huge anomaly in the person of a player I will just refer to as *"Big Joe."* Big Joe towered above any other player on the entire squad at six feet four inches and tipping the scales at around two hundred and fifty pounds. The coaches were ecstatic.

Big Joe worked hard as did most of our kids who were no strangers to strenuous work, sweat and sometimes pain. He was a fun kid to be around, yet he was non-assuming and quite frankly, a bit shy for someone his size. Joe's grasp of the English language was spotty at times, but like the other migrant students, he worked hard to improve those skills as well. On one particular day, the coaches were putting the finishing touches on our kicking teams, and the time had arrived to find a player to be our kicker on these special teams. We needed someone to handle kickoffs, extra points and field goals. Since it was early season and our knowledge of the various skill sets among the players was still coming into focus, we opened the tryouts to any team member who wanted to give it a shot. I served as the special teams' coach, so it became my charge to weed through the hopefuls who were auditioning and find that one shining star.

To say that the auditions were considerably less than impressive would be a huge understatement of the situation. Player after player would shank the kicks left or right or dribble the ball a few yards down the field. It was at this point, as my frustration mounted in this process, that one player came to me and told me, *"Coach, you need to see Big Joe kick."* Now Joe had not even stepped up for the tryouts, but at this point we certainly had nothing to lose. I spoke with Joe briefly and he confirmed that he could kick the ball a considerable distance, but only did it for fun out in his yard killing time.

I ushered Big Joe over to the teed-up pigskin and asked him to give me a demonstration of his skills. Joe backed off about five yards, took a running start and kicked the ball about fifty yards high and deep down the field. My eyes opened wide and my heart raced as I watched the ball sail down the field. Wow! Hoping that this was not a one-time performance, I quickly teed the ball up again for a second kick. Second verse, same as the first; Big Joe nailed another kick high and deep. The scene was repeated another ten times and I was sold. Big Joe was our man.

With the auditions closed, the time had come to put our entire kickoff team on the field and practice our coverage of Joe's kicks. Part of coaching a kicker involves making them aware of the guidelines and instructions from the game officials about putting the ball in play. This included where to spot the tee, etc. I looked Big Joe square in the eyes and instructed him to align himself behind the ball and that I would play the part of the game official to simulate a game situation. I informed Joe that once both teams were lined up, he had to wait for the official to point to him and blow his whistle before he could approach and kick the ball. Joe nodded his understanding of my instructions, so we were ready to go.

With all our team poised and in position, I pointed to Joe and blew my whistle to signal him that it was time to put that big foot into action. As he had done many times in our tryouts, Joe approached the ball on a run. This time, however, the ball squirted about ten yards down the field spinning around on the ground like a top. No problem; a fluke. I retrieved the ball, and we set the scene again knowing that Joe must have taken his eye off the ball momentarily. We lined up again and Joe was poised to kick. Again, I pointed to him and blew my whistle to initiate the start of play. I was prepared to see the kick travel the field and land in the end zone, when once again I witnessed a skipping, rolling, spinning kick that quite frankly Joe's little sister could have performed better.

I was puzzled and quite honestly dumbfounded by what was going on. Where had the Big Joe, who had drilled kick after kick into the end zone in tryouts, disappeared to? There must be some simple coaching adjustment that I needed to make for him to regain that form. Again, I scooped up the ball and brought it back to Joe to tee up for yet another attempt. Being one who seizes the coachable moments, I looked at Joe and spoke with the intent to encourage. I asked him, in a calm yet concerned tone, if there was a problem. His response almost dropped me to my knees in both shock and laughter that I remember to this day.

All six feet four and two hundred and fifty pounds of Big Joe looked at me and in his broken English told me with a serious and troubled look, *"Coach, that whistle scares me!"* In a game in which every play begins and ends with a whistle blowing, this was not a good thing. How do you coach the fear of whistles out of someone? I had found a kicker that would be rendered useless by the simple sound of a whistle putting the ball into play. It was a landmark moment for me and my learning curve as well--not about football, but about the simple power of fear.

I'm still not sure to this day what in Joe's life to that point had given him a fear of whistles. Had his young and impressionable mind flashed back to scenes from his migrant work or his family life? That never did become apparent to me in our follow-up discussions. All I do know is that the fear generated by that sound was real for Joe, and it caused his focus and ability to perform a skill that he had demonstrated time after time to become diminished. The most elementary effects of fear had manifested itself to me through Big Joe right there on that dusty practice field in

Cotulla, Texas. This was a simple, yet well-orchestrated, demonstration of the effects that fear can have on our talents, our emotions, our lives.

My Big Joe story has a happy ending in that through many talks, explanations, practices and trial and error, Joe was able to overcome his aversion to whistles. Becoming familiar with the actual facts surrounding our fears is the first step to overcoming them. He became a decent kicker and a solid player for us that season in 1973. More than that, he learned to face his fears and to overcome this and other perceived obstacles in his life. My tenure in Cotulla lasted only one year as I was offered and accepted a more prestigious coaching position back in San Antonio. Working with Big Joe and the other wonderful kids in that tiny Texas town had given me greater insight and tools to employ in my battle against my own fears. Like President Johnson before me, I witnessed first-hand the crippling effect of poverty and discrimination. I can only hope that Big Joe used the experience in other areas of his life to push fear to the background and conquer his world.

We spend so much of our time and thoughts in life in fear of something. Fear is evident as a strong emotion that transfers to manifest itself in our mental capacities and our physical being. You most likely have heard the acronym for FEAR as False Evidence Appearing Real. I agree with this analogy to the point that things we don't understand or have a keen knowledge of, we tend to fear--hence the *"False Evidence"* claim. But does simply knowing the science behind severe apprehension about heights or tight spaces make the emotion any less real when it bubbles to the surface in our mind? We know the facts. We understand the evidence. Yet the raw emotion of fear overwhelms the reality of fact.

It is especially those things that might produce perceived failure or bodily harm to us or others that tend to ignite our fears the most. Fear is not an illusion, fantasy or lie when it swells up in our psyche as a full-blown emotion that can make us cry, shake, faint and lose all focus. I have a close friend who has a rampant fear of heights. She is highly intelligent and educated, and understands the engineering of tall buildings and the science of flying. She accepts those principles as solid evidence, but you still aren't going to quell the queasy stomach, increased heart rate, the sweaty palms and the anxious mind that shouts to her, that she and heights equal a dangerous situation. How then do we overcome some of the fears in our lives that are emotion driven and deeply seeded in our minds?

I guess if I had a solid answer for that question I could bottle it and make millions treating the neuroses and even psychoses that abound in our world. I do know this: understanding and pinpointing our fears is the first step to overcoming them. We must look at the *"why"* factor and then examine what action can be taken to become more at ease and comfortable in certain surroundings and situations. This is not something that has been proven easy to do alone and often requires a good deal of discussion, introspection and even psychotherapy. Extreme and recurring fear needs attention from a wide variety of fronts in the ongoing battle to push aside those emotional demons that often hang over us.

Our fear of physical injury serves us as a protective mechanism that rushes to the forefront and assist us in making us more cautious and keeping us safe. We have learned, or been witness to, that certain things and certain situations may lead to harm, pain or even death. We educate ourselves about certain dangers and make every effort to steer clear of those things and situations accordingly. But what do we do about an emotional fear of failure? What about the fear of speaking in public; the fear of not getting the job; the fear of not being accepted by your family or a romantic interest; or the fear of disappointing someone dear to you in life? These fears are no less real and damaging to finding the ultimate happiness and fulfillment in our lives than those of physical danger. The question then becomes what can we do in our lives to identify, neutralize and overcome our fears?

Fear is our mind and emotions pushing us forward to answer the situational questions that we may confront several times each day: "What *will happen next?*" This is the critical point where the imagination versus education effect can stir the fire of our fears and rattle our psyche, rendering us an emotional mess. In a blink of an eye our fears can subside or manifest into fruition. The central issue is how we learn to recognize and read our fears, determine fact from fantasy, assess the actual threat level, and respond in the appropriate manner. I know. This is much easier said than done.

How then can we learn to recognize and deal proactively with our fears? Let's visit a sweet and simple lesson from the Disney classic film, *Monsters, Inc.* This animated jewel centers upon the fear that most of us encounter as a child that monsters are lurking in the closet and under our beds. I'm not sure exactly where that type of fear has root in our early life experiences, but most all of us have experienced it. In the movie, it is the presumed duty of the monsters to scare us and thus interrupt our peace, happiness and sense of security.

The prime monster character in the movie is a giant furry blue monster named Sulley. Sulley excels at scaring children with his monster roar, but is a gentle giant by nature. Boo, the precocious and courageous little three-year-old character has a different perception of Sulley. She sees him as a big fluffy blue cat that she chooses to call *"Kitty"*. Boo embraces Sulley rather than fearing him and, through the process and her ove and laughter, softens the heart of the monster. Her lack of fear not only changes Sulley, but it becomes the tipping point that changes the entire monster world. Overcoming our fears presents us with the opportunity to open the door to a new awareness of peace, love and happiness in our world too, just as it did for Boo and Sulley.

How then do we attack our fears? As I mentioned previously, we must first identify our fears and search for an understanding as to what might be the trigger for the fear, and why it persists in holding our emotions hostage. The simple strategy of sharing and discussing our fears with others can often lead to an epiphany of our way out of that bondage. We can learn to identify a regiment of activities that allows us to basically practice at working through our fear and situational anxiety. We can strengthen our emotional muscles. We can learn to fight through the storm and into the sunlight on the other side. We must ask ourselves if there is something that we can consciously do to decrease the fear or anxiety in a particular situation. If so, then we need to work through those processes.

In athletics, we call the time used to practice various segments of a game when the pressure and anxiety might be at the highest level, *"situational practice."* By practicing under the simulated pressure circumstances, we are able to train our mind and bodies to be more at ease if and when those situations present themselves in an actual game. We can do the same thing in our personal lives by being part of a focus group, engaging in a mastermind gathering, or simply having an accountability partner to share and talk through our fears and challenges. The greater we are acquainted with our own fears, the more we study them, understand them, share them and practice the antidote, the greater our probability of escaping those binding shackles.

All-time basketball great Michael Jordan stated that, *"Limits, like fear, are often an illusion."* The only reality is in the life that we choose to breathe into those fears. Dale Carnegie shared, *"You can conquer almost any fear if you will only make up your mind to do so. For remember, fear doesn't exist anywhere except in the mind."* Fear is a powerful emotion, but it only manifests itself if we give energy and life to the thoughts that support it. If we choose to sit alone in our fear it will eventually consume our time, energy and zeal for living a meaningful and gratifying life.

Live your life in a smart and secure manner that helps to diminish the fear factors. Recognize and identify your fears, and attack the root source that may be generating your fear-laden thoughts. Share your fears with trusted family and friends in an effort to bring them into the light and out of the dark corners of your mind. I encourage you to take to heart the lesson of Big Joe and don't let the whistle scare you out of a full life. Line yourself up, wait for it to be blown and then take a running start and kick your fears deep down the field.

Lesson Five

Solidify Your Goals- It's Hard to Hit a Moving Target

> *"Our goals are only personal when we engage and take ownership of them. Sometimes, in our humanness, we don't really know and understand in the moment what is meant for our greater good in the future."*
>
> **Fred Clausen**

As I have stared down the many forks in the roads of my life, the ultimate challenge has been to find the path that ran parallel with my dreams and goals. The balancing act in defining those goals is that our goals are often a moving target in our early years as we search to find our personal identity and match it with our perceived mission in life. Many times in life, we toss around the notion of goals and dreams. All too often we give more lip service than time to developing goals, which coincide with our conscious desire to both achieve and to make a difference. Goals give us the direction to move down our life path and provide the *"what"* in our game plan. I love this quote from an unknown author that relates, *"Your dreams are just your dreams until you write them down…then they become your goals."*

Where are our desires and goals born? We all have the seeds of greatness and accomplishment hard wired into our being. Some of us have a higher level of intensity and drive to accompany our goals, and our goals are as varied as we are as human beings. Others approach all of life with a more laid-back demeanor and drive. Hence, we develop and display different personality types. All goals originate in our thoughts and conscious intentions to achieve something at some level to meet the needs that we have identified in our mind. Whether you possess a high-energy or low-key approach to the pursuit of your goals, we all want to accomplish things even if on a variety of levels.

Our goals are born from our thoughts, and our thoughts produce a visual production of what we perceive our accomplishments should be and look like when manifested. No one can provide you with a goal, with reasonable expectation of achievement, unless you have bought into the vision and the road map for success. Goals need to be specific much like the blueprint for a construction project. The more detailed we are in our efforts, the more likely we are to achieve goals which closely resemble those that have sprung from our conscious thoughts and imagination.

Athletic events have goals or goal lines that must be reached or accomplished to score. Seems too silly to even imagine a football, basketball or soccer game without them doesn't it? Yet, many times people, teams, corporations, and organizations push through their daily routines with no specific definable goals in mind. There is no level to be achieved, no award to be strived for that is clearly in focus for all of those involved. An individual or organization without clearly defined goals is equivalent to riding a merry-go-round. You are in motion, traveling in circles and getting nowhere fast. The point is that the measure of success is in achieving your goals. Without well-defined goals, there is no tangible way to determine or measure your growth and progress. Defining our goals allows us to develop the all-important action game plan of the *"how"* part of the equation.

As a young coach in the early 1970's, I quickly determined some base goals for my professional life. I distinctly wrote down that I wanted to be a head football coach at the highest level of competition in Texas high school football. I wanted to win a state championship. I wanted to coach the Texas High School All-Star football game and I wanted to become President of the Texas High School Coaches Association. These were some very lofty goals, but I figured that I should set the bar high. I was high energy and ambitious. I found that if you don't set your own goals in life, you will most likely end up working for someone else to help them achieve theirs. I wrote these specific goals down and read over them many times as I moved through my career.

I'm sure that you might be curious to know how many of those specific goals I have been able to achieve. The answer is very few as they were originally written. However, the impetus provided to my life and career did not provide me those specific goals, but something even better. I became a successful head football coach and experienced a great deal of success as a top assistant as well; but not at the highest level in Texas. I did however become an Athletic Director for a large school district at the highest level, overseeing nine schools and over one hundred and fifty coaches. I never won a state championship but had numerous big playoff wins. I did realize the thrill of coaching in the 1993 Texas High School All-Star football game. I never became the President of the Texas High School Coaches Association, but in 2008, I was elected the President of the prestigious Texas High School Athletic Directors Association; the largest interscholastic state association in the country. All of these achievements were hybrids of my original goals list from 1973, my first year in coaching.

Often when we establish our goals, and even when we seek divine intervention, we limit ourselves by only seeking specific things that we deem important to us and in our limited vision of the overall picture in life. The dynamics of life are constantly changing. I've learned to share with God and the universe by praying that I be granted or allowed to achieve a particular request or *"something better."* Why put limits on yourself and the energy around your goals? It took me a while to understand the reasoning behind the

Garth Brooks' song, *"I Thank God for Unanswered Prayers."* Sometimes, in our humanness, we don't really know and understand in the moment what is meant for our greater good in the future. We assume we know today what will be in our long-term best interest. Many times, we awaken a few years down the road giving thanks that some of those wants and wishes did not come to fruition. The energy and dynamics of life provide us a surprising and suspenseful ride. Keep the channels open to receive the greater good in life.

We tend to put limits upon our own potential at times. The simple truth is that my thoughts and words shouldn't impose self-inflicted limits on my own power or that of God and the universe. Limited thinking will produce limited results. There may be much more headed my way if I am open to it. There is an old athletic saying that says, *"Shoot for the stars. If you fall a little short, you'll still end up in the clouds towering above most of the rest."* Singer Jimmy Dean once said, *"I can't change the direction of the wind, but I can adjust my sails to always reach my destination."*

Life has a way of providing twists and turns down those chosen paths from the fork in the road that challenge us to fight hard for our goals. The universe doesn't yield accolades in life without us demonstrating a strong will and determination to succeed. The strength of our commitment, and tenacity of our efforts, is directly related to the specific *"why"* that is the underlying foundation and motivation for our goals. It is in knowing your *"why"* …the deep seeded reason that you are working to achieve your goals, that will push us through the tough bumps and turns. To define your goals without determining your *"why"* is a strategy that will leave you running on empty when the times get tough.

General George S. Patton warned, *"You need to overcome the tug of people against you as you reach for high goals."* There is a human instinct at times that invites others outside of your dreams, with less drive and courage, to work against your efforts. Many times, this is unconscious sabotage to maintain the status quo. Many times, it is a bit of jealousy that can creep in from friends, co-workers and even family and can cause a drag on your efforts to excel. I call it the *"Crab Syndrome."*

Having been raised around the Gulf Coast, I saw many wash tubs filled with blue crabs in my time. If you observe carefully, some of the crabs will climb and claw over the others in their efforts to pull themselves up to the top of the tub and escape their fate of a boiling pot of water. Very few, if any make it out. Not because they can't reach, but simply because the other crabs will latch on to them and pull them back down. Thus, we have the definition of the *"Crab Syndrome."* How many times in our life do we hear those snide comments that try to discourage us and pull us back down from our dreams and goals into the common tub of mediocrity? It's puzzling how even our closest family and friends often can't handle the reflection that they see when they look into the eyes of someone else's success.

Goals are not a *"one size fits all"* proposition. We all motor on a different frequency and energy level. We all desire different accomplishments and embrace different dreams. Our individuality is never more on display than through our personal dreams and goals. I have been witness to the damage to the human self-esteem when we are held to someone else's standards and goals that are not aligned with our own. Our dreams, desires and goals are as individual as our DNA. Unwittingly, some parents psychologically handicap their own children by trying to force them to fit their own mold, goals and accomplishments or those of an older sibling. Nothing is more demoralizing that trying to live up to someone else's goals and aspirations. Our goals are only personal when we engage and take ownership of them.

It is imperative that you strive for balance in your goals. Setting goals that are too high, or unrealistic, can lead to frustration and ultimately, failure. Setting goals that are too low will provide little challenge, foster a loss of focus, and therefore, limit the development of your full potential. Dream big, but give yourself a target that you can hit. If you expect to achieve great things, work toward your goals every day. An unknown author once said that, *"Goals are our dreams with deadlines."* Having a time line attached to your efforts is often a great motivator to keep you engaged and moving forward. Establish daily goals and celebrate small daily achievements! Enjoy the ride down the road to success. Remember, you chose this fork in the road. Why wait until the end of the trip? The most rewarding moments will come along the way.

Goals are seldom achieved without a well-established plan of action. The sequential work and achievement of small goals daily will pave the way to weekly success. Success breeds success and is a huge motivating factor. It is by achieving these short-term and intermediate goals that we move in a steady and methodical manner toward the ultimate success that we desire. There is no greater feeling than the recognition and reward of a job well done and a goal that has been accomplished. Celebrating those achievements will provide the motivation for you to strive to achieve the harder and greater quest. Human nature causes us to try harder, work longer, become more focused and determined, when we feel that what we have done well is noticed and appreciated.

I will close with a quote from American educator, minister and civil rights icon, Benjamin Elijah Mays, *"The tragedy of life doesn't lie in not reaching your goals. The tragedy lies in having no goal to reach. It isn't a calamity to die with dreams unfulfilled, but it is a calamity not to dream."*

Lesson Six

The 40 Second Clock is Ticking- Call the Play

> *"Our decisions leave a visible and traceable record of our personal priorities. Our lives are a reflection of the totality of our daily decisions and exhibit our integrity, our priorities and our spiritual values."*
>
> **Fred Clausen**

One of the most important characteristics and personal skills that a person needs to be successful is the ability to make educated, calculated and timely decisions. The ability to choose between life's infinite variables and choices in each and every facet of our lives determines our pathway and our degree of success. If you watch college or NFL football, you have undoubtedly noticed the small little time clocks located somewhere in the end zones. You see them of course on your TV screen as they tick down the forty seconds between the time one play ends and the time the next play must begin to avoid a delay of game penalty. My greatest education in decision making came from my coaching experience of having to call the next play.

What determines the choices that you make in life? Do you think with your mind or your heart or perhaps both? Are you guided by the physical world alone or does your spiritual consciousness weigh in on the choices and decisions in your life as well? These are all excellent questions and ones which we need to explore and have a genuine understanding. Each of us needs to know what factors, elements, situations and emotions play a part in our methods and practices of decision making. Growing up and becoming a mature and productive adult is not about making all the right decisions. It is rather about learning to deal with and accept the consequences of the decisions that we make. All of our decisions and actions in life originate in our thoughts and from the two ends of our conscious spectrum-- love or fear. Our challenge is to make as many decisions and take as many positive and creative actions as we can, that are born out of love.

Without decisions being made in our life, nothing happens. It is like standing at the starting line of a race in anticipation of the event and no one ever shoots the starting pistol. Life is not one huge epic adventure or one-time production. It is rather a drama series of touching emotional and meaningful moments entwined with challenges and stress that are woven together based on our choices, decisions and actions. Spirit based decisions involve a closer communication with God. We commune with God through prayer and meditation to quiet our minds and find clarity. Enlightened from the introspection, we emerge with a decisive plan and take action.

In football, calling the next play isn't just a glance at a card in the coach's hand or echoing instructions from the press box to the players. The careful decision on calling the next play has been analyzed, thought through, examined, practiced and critiqued for days leading up to an actual game. Life decisions need careful thought as well. We are responsible and accountable for the actions that are derived from our decisions. The dynamics of decision making changes drastically the more people and varied opinions that enter the equation.

I offer as an example the almost comical effort in my family to decide on a restaurant for dinner. Try as I may it is at times extremely difficult to get my lovely wife to share with me the answer to the simple question, *"Where would you like to eat tonight dear?"* Decisions, decisions! Her usual reply, *"I don't care, you decide."* The forty-second clock process has taken on a new meaning when mentioned to my wife in these intense decision-making modes of where to eat. Uttering those words to her are my last resort, but sometimes necessary.

I am, in my mind of course, the most agreeable of people when it comes to where we eat. Do they have food? Great, I'm in. To my wife however, it at times seems to become an almost painful, life or death decision. When her response indicates that I should make a decision, I usual take only an instant to offer a choice. In most cases, my first suggestion of cuisine and establishment is normally met with an abrupt, *"Oh no. They don't have anything there that I like."* I then alter my *"play call"* to offer another choice to which I normally get another head shake and raising of the eyebrow. Strike two! My last gasp effort as the clock ticks down is to again state the obvious, *"Then just tell me where you want to go."* It is after we toss my final offering around through several rounds of this process that I finally, but hesitantly launch my desperation *"Hail Mary pass"* with the words, *"Forty seconds, and the clock is ticking. Call the play!"* Now understand that this last-resort plea from me is well understood and not liked in the least by my wife. But at this point she knows that I need a decision and make it now…please!

I know that this simple illustration is a bit trite and silly. I find it a mildly humorous analogy of how we all get wrapped up in our many situations and choices in life, sometimes to the degree that we freeze when we must finally *"call the play"*. A decision is needed to jump start the action. It would be prudent and responsible of me to point out that decisions take on priority ranking in our day-to-day life. Where we eat is an afterthought as compared to which house do we buy; where do I go to college; which job do I apply for. Some decisions are almost instinctive in a habitual sort of way. Others need careful research, thought, dialogue and experimentation before we make the final call. Some decisions ride a wave of infinite time while others operate much like the ticking forty-second clock in football that demands an answer in a short window of opportunity.

We make literally thousands of decisions every hour of every day. Some of these are as trivial as the clothes we wear, while others, like driving, require a constant process of decisions to insure our safety and well being. Distracted driving is an increasing cause of car accidents. The distraction, whatever it may be, causes us to not receive or be aware of vital changing information ahead. Therefore, our ability to make a decision to alter our course, slow our speed or engage in an evasive maneuver is diminished. The autonomic nervous system of our body runs many of our body functions on autopilot. We don't have to decide to breathe or have our heart beat or our blood to flow. We do however, have to decide how we care for and nourish our bodies through our free-will nutrition and lifestyle choices. Our life literally hinges daily on the decisions that we choose to make in almost every segment of our existence.

My all-time-favorite baseball player and character is the famous 1950's catcher of the New York Yankees, Yogi Berra. Yogi was not only a Hall of Fame player, but he was also the originator of many zany, yet thought provoking statements. My favorite *"Yogism"* was based loosely on directions and decisions when he uttered, *"When you come to the fork in the road, take it!"* On the surface you just want to chuckle and scratch your head. You might even say, *"Well, which way?"*, to which I'm sure Yogi's reply would have been, *"exactly."* The point to me is that when faced with the many *"forks in the road"* of life, we have to make a decision and pick the one on which we will travel. We can stand and wait at the fork as life passes by, or we can make a decision and see where the chosen path leads.

Lee Iacocca, famous automobile executive and pioneer of the Ford Mustang stated, *"Even a correct decision is wrong when it was taken too late."* You can't decide to catch the train once it has left the station. The greatest single hindrance to timely decision making is the fear that you will make the wrong decision. Every great achievement began with the decision to try...to take educated, calibrated action. Truly successful decision making is a balance between our knowledge, our instinct and our courage. The more knowledge we have about a situation or problem, the narrower our margin for error will be in making and implementing our decision. Sometimes our past experiences, our character, our passion will guide us to instinctively make the correct decisions. Nothing is a sure thing in life. We must exemplify the courage to step into our decisions and see them through while at the same time having the fortitude to deal with the consequences.

Life does not always afford us time to ponder our decisions as they come at us in rapid fire order all day long. In the arena where we do have the opportunity and time to ponder our decisions and actions, a proven strategy is good to have in mind. The best model that I have found for making good decisions follows much the same script as the scientific method of problem solving. First, you must identify the problem and decision to be made. Second, you must research and gather information and form well thought- out options. This allows you to identify the potential positives and negatives of each option. Third, and most important, make the decision and take action. Fourth and finally, evaluate your results; reflect on your process and adjust where needed to fine tune. This method is adaptable to the simplicity or complexity of your situation and need.

It is important to keep in mind that decisions that will have a wide-reaching impact on others should provide the stakeholders with an opportunity to have input in the decision-making process. Notice I said, *"the opportunity to have input."* I did not necessarily imply a vote on the final decision. Prudent decision making at higher levels often requires the leadership, or leadership team, to make the final decisions based on all the information that has been presented and options examined. It is the leadership that is charged in most cases with the implementation of large and impactful decisions. President Harry Truman had a famous sign that adorned his desk in the oval office that said, *"The Buck Stops Here!"* The meaning of that was that once a problem came up the chain to him for a decision, there was nowhere else for it to go, no one else to turn to, no standing any longer at the fork in the road. He had to make the call.

Decisions need to come from a place of integrity and for the greater good. Our decisions leave a visible and traceable record of our personal priorities. Our lives are a reflection of the totality of our daily decisions and exhibit our integrity, our priorities and our spiritual values. We co-create our own reality each day as we interact with the world, God and the universe. Stephen Covey wrote, *"We are the creative force of our own life, and through our own decisions rather than our conditions, we can learn to do those things vital to accomplish our goals."* We should use past decisions that did not turn out well as learning experiences and guide post for future decisions. Just as a coach will not always call a successful play, we do not always make the right and perfect decisions.

The essential lesson is that we grow wiser and more aware of the possible impact as we make our decisions. We strive to add to our arsenal of knowledge and experience that then allows us greater insight and awareness as we make future decisions. Experience provides us with an in-your-face lesson on how the well known economic principle of *"opportunity cost"* applies to our everyday lives. *"Opportunity cost"* is the principle that states if you decide to do one thing, or spend your money on something, then, along with the monetary value exchanged, the cost is also whatever opportunity you gave up in order to have or do that thing. Deciding for option A, means we give up the chance or opportunity for option B. This is one of the most important considerations we must learn on the path to becoming a prudent and decisive decision maker.

This *"opportunity cost"* factor, while beneficial in our decision considerations, can also trigger a stagnating emotional and mental block in our decision process. This block is often referred to as the *"fear of loss"*. *"Fear of loss"* can become a double-edged sword in decision making. If we make a decision based on what we might lose, rather than what we might gain, then we often sit on the fence and never pick the path at the fork in the road. If this *"fear of loss"* emotional factor weighs too heavily on our decisions, we may tend to make decisions too quickly, and ones that are not founded in our knowledge and understanding.

Decisions that involve matters of the heart and deep seeded emotions need to be congruent with the information and situation that guides us. Love and our emotional consciousness can at times alter our vision and ability to clearly evaluate a situation. We must be cautious not to let our emotions override the information and lure us into making decisions that feel good for the moment but are not built on solid knowledge and common sense. Many times, we must make decisions with limited time and knowledge. It is during these moments that we must draw from our past experiences and our basic intuition. The litmus test of any decision that must be made quickly and with limited information, should center upon the good or possible harm that might arise from the consequences and impact of the decision.

Let's look at an entertaining example of how rapid and emotional decision making, without solid information and with the added element of *"fear of loss,"* can lead to a scenario fit for Hollywood. In the classic movie, *Runaway Bride*, Maggie Carpenter, played by Julia Roberts, is a spirited and attractive young woman who has left a trail of destruction at the altar of love. She enters relationships frequently and inevitably is blinded by the emotional rush of new love. Time after time she rapidly succumbs to the initial lure of romance and marriage, only to balk and bolt at the ceremony. Maggie's panic mode is triggered by her *"fear of loss."* The loss that she fears the most is giving her heart to someone else when she hasn't even discovered her own identity.

The basic flaw in Maggie's love and marriage decision making process is the lack of knowledge of her own emotional and spiritual identity. Confusion abounds. Her romantic interest flip flops as often as her preference in how she likes her eggs cooked. Sometimes, as with Maggie's story, decisions of the heart can only come into focus when we first have a solid grasp of our own wants, needs and dreams. Knowing and loving yourself is paramount to being able to love someone else.

A decision that involves changing yourself or your values for someone else is often unsettling and damaging to our self image. You can't share yourself until you know yourself. As you may know, the *Runaway Bride* story ends with Maggie finding herself and realizing her sense of self worth. Her value is not tied or bound to the love or acceptance of someone else. This revelation in her life eases her anxiety and allows her to overcome the fear of losing herself in the process. Of course, it helped that Richard Gear's character was her final suitor.

There is one given in our never-ending quest in making decisions in life. If we don't step up and engage in making decision for ourselves, someone else will make them for us. By not becoming a decision maker, we are surrendering control to others. Why would we want to put our life, our job, our safety, our future exclusively in the hands of others? Courage is the underlying element that propels us into action to not only decide our own destiny, but to also engineer it and manage it ourselves. God and the universe have granted us free will and the opportunity to make decisions that will guide our way. We must make decisions that are based on the values, knowledge and life experiences that provide us a clear vision of what is good, just and loving.

Each day, as the forty second clock ticks down, we have to stand in like an NFL quarterback, survey the field, the defense, consider the situation and the stakes for all, and then make the call. We won't always call the correct play or make the right decisions. The greatest college basketball coach of all time, John Wooden, shared with us, *"Success is never final, Failure is never fatal. It is Courage that counts. Things turn out best in life for those people who make the best out of how things turn out."* Remember, every accomplishment in life begins with a thought and the decision to engage. Call your own plays. Pick your favorite restaurants. Find your right path. Discover yourself. You have the final vote on the direction, adventure and dynamics that will shape your life. Don't allow the forty second clock to run out on your hopes and dreams.

Lesson Seven

Keep Your Head on a Swivel- Awareness is Critical

> *"To find our true self and the conscious values and beliefs that we truly embrace in life is to find God within ourselves. Our heart only reflects the signals that our thoughts emit."*
>
> **Fred Clausen**

I love to just sit in places and people watch. The observation of other people and how they pass through and react with the world, their fellow man and the environment is both intriguing and entertaining to me. One of the things that I tend to observe is the awareness level, or lack thereof, that people have to their surroundings even as they move through life. We are becoming an increasingly distracted society that tends to walk through the physical world with its head down staring at electronic devices while quite oblivious to life in general. We meet with family and friends for coffee or a meal and escape the present moment into a shining screen of light in our hands that lures us to distraction.

Some people will lament that they are just becoming more knowledgeable or more informed by constantly panning CNN, ESPN or Facebook while the real-world flashes by right in front of them. Information is not awareness.

On more than one occasion, I have witnessed a person walking down the street completely focused on texting or checking something out on their cell phone unaware of their present world. I can almost predict what is about to happen to them as I observe them in relationship to the changing terrain ahead of their path. I have seen them run into poles, trash cans, other people and even walk off a curb and fall. I have witnessed them ending up in front of a screeching car like a deer caught in the headlights when their awareness returns. Distraction in any form is quite simply a loss of awareness. When we lose our awareness in the here and now, we run the calculated risk of having our world and sometimes even our bones fractured. It is imperative to creating a meaningful life for us to develop both our sense of awareness, and our ability to live from a place of consciousness. We must work to be present in the moment.

Awareness is the cornerstone of our meaningful interactions with ourselves and with the rest of the world. Drawing from my days as a football defensive coordinator, I will share with you that the foundation of any great defense is the middle linebacker. He is in the center of the action, much like we are in the center of all the actions and activities in our lives. The number one characteristics vital to successfully manning this position is awareness. The player's alignment in the center of the formations allows him to move with the flow of each play and engage in the action on almost every down. He is coached consistently to *"keep your head on a swivel."*

I'm sure this sounds a bit bizarre to those who have a limited knowledge of football. The coaching point that arises from the statement is that you must maintain a keen awareness and be constantly surveying the entire landscape, the formation, the situation and the possibilities and probabilities of what might be coming your way. The linebacker gathers constant information about the rapidly changing domain by moving his head and eyes from side to side…much like it was truly perched and rotating on a swivel. He is connected by his senses in general and his sight in particular to the ever-changing environment in front of him.

Analogous to the middle linebacker, the ability to mesh our inner knowledge and subconscious awareness with the physical awareness of the scenes unfolding in our present reality, determine our choices, actions and results. In life as in athletics, the higher your awareness, the better your choices will be. Better choices provide a higher probability of success in our life. The great poet, writer and civil rights activist Maya Angelou, shared, *"Be present in all things and thankful for all things."* Awareness in life as in football requires being awake and in tuned with the present moment and the present environment. Deepak Chopra adds, *"Awareness is the birthplace of possibility. Everything you want to do, everything you want to be starts here."*

Clueless is the name of a quirky little movie from years past about the struggles of a young girl to become more self aware. Clueless is also what we are at many stages of development in our mental, emotional and physical maturation. Clueless quite simply refers to a lack of knowledge or understanding about something or some situation. As smart and evolved as we often all profess to be, we all have our clueless moments. The starting gate to universal awareness lies in our personal quest to first find self awareness. It is only by first knowing ourselves that we can expand our search for knowledge and awareness to the universe. I would like to delve into several main areas of awareness that I personally believe are the most vital to our happiness and fulfillment in life.

Self awareness is our ability to know and understand ourselves. Our self awareness is greatly dependent on the knowledge and experience that we receive through the cornerstones of our sensory awareness, our emotional awareness and our social awareness. In our efforts to live in the present and in awareness, we must begin with our continual quest to become self aware. Self awareness is having the clear perception of your own personality, including strengths, weaknesses, thoughts, beliefs, motivation and emotions. Humans are unique in that we actually have the ability to be aware of our awareness. We also should have a conscious understanding of perception awareness, or how we may be perceived by others through our words and actions. We often view ourselves in quite a different light than others in our life.

Self awareness allows us to understand other people in context of how they perceive us and our attitudes and responses as they relate to them in the moment. We all perceive and understand things in a different context unless we share our own awareness specifically. Being self aware should also mean that I can detect when someone else is not on the same page with me in a particular moment and is essentially clueless on a particular situation or topic.

Sensory awareness is best defined as our ability to focus on our recognition and interactions that are related to one of our senses. We see something. We hear something. We smell, taste or feel something. Our sensory awareness enhances our universal awareness and allows us a greater insight into our own self awareness as it relates. Through our senses we soak in our reality and make it available for us to examine in our consciousness. The sensory world provides us with a constant fact finding and detection system for our surroundings and our conscious environment. We sort through literally millions of sensory indicators each day as we move through our lives and our environment. Life was meant to be seen, smelled, touched, heard and tasted.

Emotional awareness is the knowledge and ability to recognize emotions and emotional situations in ourselves and in others. Fear, anger, joy, happiness, love, sadness, disgust, and surprise are just a few of our emotional markers. This emotional awareness allows us to discern the different feelings and guide our thinking, actions and reactions in appropriate situations. Emotional awareness of others gives us very distinct clues to the impact of our actions in real time feedback. When our words bring another person to tears, it is our emotional awareness that lets us know, within the context of those words, if the tears are from anger, sadness, joy or relief. Our emotional awareness can stretch across the human experience and spectrum of reactions.

The awareness of knowing the proper and accepted behavior and inner actions in social and even private settings is our social awareness. Our social awareness often is triggered by what we have perceived with our senses and detect through our emotional gage. To put it simply, it is our recognition of what many might call *"appropriate behavior"*, although that designation seems to be a moving target in our world today. An important lesson that I have learned is that you can never assume that your own awareness is transferred into someone else just because it is a shared situation. Even shared words can take on a different meaning if your knowledge and awareness aren't on the same wave length. Many of life's confusing moments can be avoided if we only slow down, communicate clearly and sync our thoughts with others.

I have often intermingled the terms consciousness and awareness in my thoughts and perceptions. Although they both indicate a sense of knowledge and understanding, it is difficult to provide an acceptable definition for consciousness that does not include the properties of awareness. Consciousness in a universal context and definition is the fact of awareness by the mind of itself and the world. The ancient Greek aphorism beckons us to *"know thyself"* first on the path to awareness. We know what we know because we are in touch with ourselves and the universal oneness that we call God. In the Bible book of Exodus, God responds to Moses' inquiry as to his name, his identity, with the statement, *"I am who I am."* Expanding that context to our own lives, *"We are who we are."* It is up to us to search, study and solve that riddle.

As with Moses, we seek to find the identity of our spiritual self. We yearn to have an answer to the mystery of, *"Who am I and why am I here?"* It is through a deep sense of introspection that we work to develop our minds, our self awareness and thus our universal spiritual awareness. This spiritual awareness allows us to recognize our being and surpass our ego self to bring us into a universal consciousness of love and oneness with God and the universe. Our two greatest challenges as humans are to become self aware and through that, find our path to spiritual awareness.

Finding our spiritual self is a process that requires much effort and time spent alone with ourselves in thought. We have the need and the hunger to explore our deep seeded thoughts and feelings and to work to discover their origins. We must answer the *"Who am I?"* question before we can answer the *"Why am I here?"* portion. Much of this work required in finding both our self awareness and our spiritual self involves prayer and meditative time. We must make a deeper connection with ourselves and with God. The high energy and hustle and bustle of everyday life is not conducive to the interconnection to our consciousness and our self awareness. It is when we quiet our minds and open our hearts that we are most likely to find the truth of our purpose and existence.

Discovering our oneness requires a certain amount of just becoming one with the universe; with nature; with infinite wisdom; with God. Free yourself from the hectic world and find yourself in the quiet and solitude of a walk in the woods, sitting by the ocean or being lost in the dreams of finding figures in the clouds overhead. The search for our self awareness can take us beautiful places. There are many paths to travel and sacred traditional activities that have been designed to bring us closer to the understanding of not just life in general, but our own life in particular.

None of our physical or worldly identifications are an accurate portrait of who we are. We are not our jobs, our titles, our cars, our clothes, our social status or our money. We are a spiritual being going through a human experience. To find our true self and the conscious values and beliefs that we truly embrace in life is to find God within ourselves. Our hearts only reflect the signals that our thoughts emit.

The Bible verse below s used at many weddings to signify the universal meaning of love as it pertains to marriage and relationships. I offer it in these writings as a testimony to the most essential element of what our spiritual awareness and our self awareness should be. God is everywhere and in everything. We are one with God. God is love, so therefore we are also love.

"Love is patient, love is kind. It does not envy, it does not boast, it is not proud. It is not rude, it is not self-seeking, it is not easily angered, it keeps no record of wrongs. Love does not delight in evil but rejoices with the truth. It always protects, always trusts, always hopes, always perseveres." —1 Corinthians 13:4-7

The Beatles' John Lennon urged us all to *"Imagine"* a world ruled by love, peace and brotherhood. How wonderful and powerful it would be if all of humanity operated from a foundation and awareness of love. Love is the central theme and the core of the teachings of all the great spiritual masters. In our own journey to self awareness the foundation of every thought, word and action should be grounded in love. In 1985 the group Huey Lewis and The News recorded their hit single, *"The Power of Love."* The first verse below provides a powerful image:

"The power of love is a curious thing
Make one man weep, make another man sing,
Change a hawk to a little white dove
More than a feeling that's the power of love."

Love is the most transformative emotion, feeling, thought and expression for us to use as the measuring stick of our deep spiritual and self awareness. Can you love yourself? Can you love your neighbor? Can you love your enemies? Can you love nature and the environment? If we fill our minds and hearts with unconditional love, then hate, fear and evil will have no place to exist. Living in love and the here and now--in the moment, requires us to focus on increasing our awareness. We must think about what we think about. As confusing as that may sound, we must simply be aware of the thoughts that we think. Why did we think that thought? Where did it originate? What in my experiences led me to think that particular thought?

As humans, we are quite unique in this mental capacity. It is the times of solitude that I spend with me, myself and I, that I can search my thoughts to discover the deep seeded areas of their origins. In my search for self awareness, I have the ability to go within and explore my core beliefs and values as they relate to my knowledge, family background, experiences and dreams. By analyzing and understanding my thoughts, I can truly become more self aware. I can work to refine my thoughts to bring myself into alignment with my spiritual self. The necessary component to changing ourselves and our consciousness lies in understanding our thoughts and refining our awareness. Awareness allows us to peek behind the curtain at OZ...to have a deeper recognition of the man in the mirror...to pull back the veil that reveals our conscious and spiritual self.

When someone says, *"I'm not the same person that I was twenty years ago,"* it is because they have altered and refined their thoughts and thus their self and spiritual awareness. Stephen Covey shared, *"Every human has four endowments; self awareness, conscience, independent will and creative imagination. These give us the ultimate human freedom…the power to choose, to respond, and to change."* I encourage you to keep your head, mind, consciousness and awareness on a swivel. Life and living in the moment, in the present, comes at us from all angles. The more aware we are, the more in tune we are with God, the universe and humanity, the greater our opportunity to live a full, meaningful and joyful life.

Lesson Eight

Without Honor, No One Wins- Integrity is Paramount

> *"Life provides us with watershed moments to gage where we are in our quest for living a life of integrity. Our response to these tests is a measure of our knowledge, understanding and maturity."*
>
> **Fred Clausen**

Throughout the years of my playing and coaching career in athletics, I have seen all levels of success and defeat. I have sat on the mountaintop of championships and slid into the valley of loss and despair. Win or lose the one characteristic that is the most cherished of all is one's integrity and reputation. Michael S. Josephson, the founder and president of the Character Counts Coalition, has a wonderful statement in poster form that has hung on my office wall for many years. It is quite simply, *"There is No Victory without Honor."* The Character Counts Coalition provides character training in many schools and athletic programs across the nation in an effort to instill and ensure that character and honor are at the core of all our thoughts and actions.

There is a simple, yet pointed statement that one of my coaching mentors used to tell our players and staff as we entered each weekend on our own in the community. The gentle reminder of the expectation of our behavior and character was, *"Go out and do what's right, because it's right, until it feels right."* That statement from my friend and mentor Coach Don Poe still resonates with me every day. Living day to day with honor, character and integrity sounds simple, yet in fact it is one our life's greatest challenges. I have given numerous lectures and clinics on the ethics of coaching to both young coaches and seasoned veterans. The message I imparted is the same one as pointed out in the quote from Mr. Josephson. If you must win in athletics or in life by skirting the rules and acceptable ethical practices, then even a victory on the scoreboard, achieved without honor, is tainted and of little value to what matters the most.

The great lesson from the statement in, *"Doing what's right, because it's right until it feels right,"* is the inference that initially this is not going to be easy and it is not going to be comfortable. Since life throws us many temptations for shortcuts, we must ease ourselves into this comfort zone of integrity. The integrity that we exude is directly related to how we embrace this challenge in our consciousness and actions. That measure of honesty and dignity are on consistent display in our lives. I have also heard integrity defined as being, *"How you act when you know others aren't looking."* Your integrity is the direct reflection of the values that you have placed at the core of your spiritual being and are keenly part of your personality. You may fool others for a while, but you can never fool the person in your mirror.

Real integrity remains solid whether in adversity or prosperity. It does not wavier under stress or trial. It manifests itself in both words and deeds. One of the greatest barometers of our integrity lies in how we treat those in our lives from whom we have nothing to gain. How do we treat those whose presence lies on the fringes of our world? How do we treat the custodian at work, the clerk at the grocery store, a homeless person, even our pets and other of God's creatures? You see, our world is not confined to just our intimate circle of family and friends. If we live in integrity, we move into each new day with the conscious intent to be a blessing to others in some manner. It is through living a day-to-day life that embraces love, honesty and integrity that will bring us closer to our fellow man, God and the divine energy of the universe.

What is the difference between honesty and integrity? Or is there a difference? The major difference between honesty and integrity is that one may be entirely honest in their observations and comments, yet their conduct and actions reflect a lack of moral reflection and steadfastness to commitments and trustworthiness. Honesty is generally thought as one of the primary indicators of our integrity. Integrity encompasses the total measure of our moral character. I have been asked often over the years about the saying, *"Athletics Builds Character."* My response is that athletic competition in itself does not build character as represented by the stories of disgraced and fallen heroes in the sports pages and on social media. What athletics and other group and team based activities does do is provide a leader the stage and vehicle to teach character in the teachable moments of practice and competition.

My freshman year in college I learned a painful lesson about honesty. As in many college athletic programs of that time, there was an age-old ritual of hazing the new players or the *"rookies."* The upper classmen, would come to your room, overtake you and bodily pick you up, take you to the restroom, dunk you headfirst into the toilet and then flush the water around your head. This ritual was affectionately known as *"flushing."* About the third late night that I was designated to be flushed, I decided enough was enough. I fought back and in the process, grabbing and breaking a gold chain around the neck of one of the senior players. His response was to smash my nose with his fist which then set off a chain reaction of players scampering for their dorm rooms. The group scattered as I struggled to regain my feet and recover from the dazed state of affairs.

Along with a broken nose, I had another dilemma. Would I keep silent to avoid any problems for the upper classman or would I provide an honest report to my coach. After a night with little or no sleep and a tough time breathing, I decided to just let it slide. Enter the universe with a learning opportunity on honesty designed specifically for me. After my morning classes, I was summoned to the head baseball coach's office. As I sat down for the visit, I was determined not to snitch on the player who had hit me. My coach looked at me and said, *"I heard there was a fight in the dorm last night on your floor. Were you or any of the other baseball players involved?"* The window was open to tell the truth, but I elected to remain steadfast in my decision. I calmly, but dishonestly assured my coach that neither I nor any other players were involved.

What I was not aware of was that the player who had hit me was so worried that I would run to the coach and tell, that he had confessed the whole incident earlier. Coach was testing me to see if, when provided the opportunity, I would be honest and truthful. He opened the trap door. I fell in. Having been caught in a lie to your coach during your first semester of your college baseball career was not a good thing. My punishment, after having my butt chewed and being lectured to, was to have to run one hundred laps around the baseball field in the next two days. The other player met the same fate for his part in the incident. Have you ever had to run a hundred laps around a baseball field with three feet of gauze crammed up each nostril of a broken nose? I can assure you that it is not conducive to being able to breathe and run at the same time. Lesson learned: Honesty, although painful at times, is always the best policy.

John C. Maxwell wisely shared with us, *"Image is what people think we are; Integrity is what we really are."* I want to take you back a few years and share a story of a thirty-eight-year-old coach who had taken his family on a much-anticipated vacation to the beach in Florida. This story helps bring into focus the relationship of honesty to integrity. This coach, as with most teachers, was of modest income and means so vacation time and money were highly treasured. After stashing away dollars monthly during the year, he finally saved up enough to load up the wife and kids and head to the beach for some family fun in the sun. After a couple of days at the beach, the kids became slightly bored and restless as kids will do. It just so happened that right across from the beach was a huge water park with rides, slides and of course the lazy river for Mom and Dad to drift around. So off went the family to the water park for the day, even though the cost of the day was steep and not in the original plan or budget. The sun peeked in and out behind the billowy Florida clouds and everyone was having a wonderful time.

    The universe has a unique manner of tossing tests our way just to keep us on our toes and to measure our resolve on certain matters. This is especially true about our honesty and integrity. The coach was having a relaxing day watching the kids enjoy the change of venue while deep down he was a bit stressed about the extra debt the experience placed on his credit card. As he coasted along that relaxing stream he noticed a Ziploc baggy float by and bump up against his inner tube. Instinctively he reached down and plucked it out of the chlorinated water. What he saw as he examined it was a wad of cash, with the visible outside wrap being a one-hundred-dollar bill. Boom! It was integrity test time.

As the coach opened the baggy and further examined the remaining contents, he discovered not just one hundred, but six hundred dollars wrapped around a drivers license ID card. Integrity--what you do when no one else is looking--remember? Here in the manmade stream was a monetary bonanza, especially in the 1980's. Six hundred dollars would pay for almost half of the vacation and would certainly mean that he could even do more fun things for the family and in greater style for the rest of the vacation. The coach eyed the ID that clearly spelled out that the baggy, money and ID belonged to someone and had somehow been lost in their trip to the water park. It was decision time. Would he keep the money and pretend not to know that it had a rightful owner, or would he exhibit great honesty and integrity and turn it in? Life provides us with watershed moments to gauge where we are in our quest for living a life of integrity. Our response to these tests is a measure of our knowledge, understanding and maturity.

I'm sorry to say that the coach chose to keep the money and only leave the ID in the baggy on a counter for it to be found by a worker from the park. I'm even sorrier to relay that the coach who exhibited this total lack of honesty and integrity was me. I gave into those human instincts that provide us with challenges and test. I failed miserably. In thinking back, there was no rhyme or reason for the poor decision on my part other than choosing greed over integrity.

Any weak thoughts of attempted justification did not sit well with my consciousness and spiritual awareness. The extra items bought with the money were a drop in the bucket, yet I had easily relinquished one of my most valuable assets--my integrity. Like the infomercials say, *"But wait, there's more!"* I was only getting warmed up on this lesson in reality being administered by the universe. I had generated some bad karma around money and prosperity in my life and at some point that would have to be reconciled.

As I returned to school that fall, anything and everything in our home that could break or fall apart did just that. The bills quickly began to add up as I wrote check after check far exceeding my six hundred dollars of ill gained windfall. The biggest check by far was hypothetically and metaphorically to the universe for the lesson on my honesty and integrity. In the book of Galatians, the Bible tells us, *"As you sow, so shall you reap."* The universe and karma serve to back God's word to the hilt on this axiom. It wasn't that I didn't know and consciously understand the right thing to do in the situation that I shared. I simply chose in the moment to ignore all that I should have embraced and held dear to both the perception and the reality of my actions and myself.

We will always have tests of our integrity in life. How we respond will greatly affect our self awareness, our spiritual awareness and our reputation in our own eyes and in the eyes of others. I have replayed this experience mentally in the past thirty years as a reminder of the price that must be paid when our honesty and integrity aren't aligned with our correct values and expectations. Our integrity may fall into the valley, but we can also pull ourselves back into balance and use the knowledge and experience for our long-term good.

I have tried diligently to do as Jesus taught in the New Testament book of John when he directed to, *"Go and sin no more."* I'm sure I have not been perfect in this quest, but I now have a solid resolve and more distinct and steadfast values on being honest and acting from integrity. I make honesty and integrity the primary goal in my dealings, conversations and relationships. Our mission is not to be perfect, but rather to strive to keep ourselves on the right path and the shortest route to living a life of integrity. Much like the GPS in our automobiles, we will at times have to *"redirect"* our route to put us back on course. Part of living in integrity is being able to recognize when we are straying slightly off course and then being able to extract strength and courage from our values and spiritual awareness to bring ourselves back into alignment. Words from Mahatma Gandhi provide me a mantra to live by, *"I will have the moral courage to make my actions consistent with my knowledge of right and wrong."*

Former first lady, Michelle Obama shared the following, *"We learn about honesty and integrity--that the truth matters...that you don't take shortcuts or play by your own set of rules...and success only counts when you earn it fair and square."* As with many aspects of our life, we can't linger in the gray area of truth and integrity. These issues are mostly black and white. We must honor the truth and approach our thoughts and actions with full integrity. We must operate from a position that instills trust in our decisions and the underlying thoughts and reasons behind our actions. We must guard our reputation diligently, for once it is lost or damaged, it is nearly impossible to reclaim. I will end by sharing this insightful quote from an unknown author who beckons us to, *"Live your life in such a way, that when people think of honesty and integrity, that they think of you."* The deepest joy and satisfaction of victory in any arena of life can only exist for those who earn it with courage, honor and integrity.

Lesson Nine

Your Greatest Trophy- The Prosperity of Life

> *"It is up to us to tap into the abundance of life and claim it for ourselves and to share the excess that flows to us with the rest of God's creations. I grow rich through sharing my prosperity, not by hoarding it."*
>
> **Fred Clausen**

I love this quote from Wayne Dyer as he shared, *"When I chased after money, I never had enough. When I centered my life on purpose and focused on giving of myself and everything that arrived into my life, then I was prosperous."* Wayne Dyer, like many famous personalities and athletes had ridden the adrenalin-filled wave of fame and wealth that eventually dumped him and the others into a dark sea of discontent. He discovered that life began in earnest when his prosperity consciousness shifted from himself to the service of others. What is your definition of prosperous? Does it rest in your bank account? Perhaps it revolves around the material possession that you have: your home, your job, your car, your club membership.

We each have our own definition of what we consider prosperity to be. My personal definition has changed over the years and will most likely continue to evolve as I age. Prosperity is as much a state of mind as it is a state of our finances and net worth. True prosperity is gleaned from the many aspects of our life that we often take for granted in the blind ignorance of our youthful follies. We often draw from life experiences, TV advertisements and social media hype to provide us with a snapshot of what prosperity should look like. We fall into the widely cast net of bigger is better; the more the merrier; the grass is greener; we want it all and we want it now.

I want to offer for your consideration that prosperity comes to us in many forms, and that true prosperity cannot be defined by wealth alone. Those who consider themselves prosperous have generally learned along the way to show gratitude for what they already have as they work to achieve even greater things. Prosperity is a mindset that is driven by the positive expectation of abundance in the world and in the universe. Before one-dollar flows into our hands, the positive attitude of our self-worth must be aligned with our expectations, dreams and ultimately our actions. The master teacher Jesus shared with us, *"For it is easier for a camel to go through the eye of a needle than for a rich man to enter the kingdom of God."*

There are many ways to interpret those words, but the one that I personally favor is that if we become lost and fixated on obtaining riches and fame alone, then our focus will not be on those things that can bring us true peace and happiness. If we lose ourselves in the constant pursuit of wealth to the detriment of love and service to the world and our fellow man, what have we gained? I'm sure you've also heard the statement that, *"Money is the root of all evil."* We live in a universe of great abundance. Money and wealth in itself doesn't necessarily give birth to evil ways. It is most often the extreme greed and lack of awareness in the other prosperity-driven areas of our lives that lead us into the temptation of evil. The will, drive and determination for success is not a breeding ground for deceitful deeds unless we allow our hunger for material wealth to over run our integrity, character and spiritual awareness.

Ponder with me for a few moments those things in your life and mine that are characteristics of true, meaningful and lasting prosperity. I will offer four areas as the basis of all prosperity with those being inclusive of our financial well being; our health; our relationships and our ambitions or goals. I will paint you a picture of how true prosperity can only come by the blending and intermingling of each of these areas. Can we be truly prosperous simply by having money yet being constantly ill and friendless? Can we reach our goals of fortune and fame without the support of family and a sound mind and body? Author Bryant McGill said, *"You cannot isolate yourself into prosperity."* We need education, dedication and cooperation with the world to become prosperous. We need to examine how our thoughts can manifest into the achievement of our personal and financial goals in life. We need to strive to know and understand the symbiotic relationships that we must embrace to become both self aware and self fulfilled. Bob Dylan's epic song, *"Like A Rolling Stone,"* provided us with a peek into the despair of those who might place all their happiness on the materialistic things of this world. The chorus of the song echoes the psychological shift from riches to rags and loneliness.

"How does it feel, How does it feel?
To be on your own, with no direction home
A complete unknown, like a rolling stone."

The revered motivational speaker and author Zig Ziglar shared with us, *"You can have anything in life that you want if you will just help enough other people get what they want."* If we only chase after money, then money is the only possible end to our pursuit. If we reach deeper into our mind and consciousness we can have whatever we can dream. It is by losing our focus on the greater good in life that we lose our way and eventually our self to the selfish and self-serving demons that lie in wait. The ancient philosopher Aristotle observed, *"Men create gods after their own image, not only with regard to their form but with regard to their mode of life."* It is when our material things become our image of God and the altar at which we choose to worship, that we teeter on the brink of disaster.

As a coach, I have followed many professional athletes, who by all stretches of the imagination had the world by the tail. They had money, they had fame, and they lived a life of opulence and excess. Most also had a posse of pseudo friends who only wanted some of their money and a piece of the action and excitement. I have been baffled by the number of these wealthy and gifted athletes who had so much disrespect for their prosperity and for themselves, that they eventually squandered both their fame and their fortunes to end up penniless. True prosperity involves having a reverence for how you share your riches, your talent and yourself. Jesus tells us in the Sermon on the Mount, Matthew 6:21, *"For where your treasure is, there your heart will be also.* In Mark 8:36 he also asks, *"For what shall it profit a man, if he shall gain the whole world, and lose his soul?"* Too many times we lose our way and our priorities about what are the most important things in our lives. Too often, the costs are dear.

I spoke earlier about the relationship between prosperity and our health. Let's do a little math around that particular topic. If I am wealthy but not healthy, then a great deal of my fortune will then be spent in the pursuit of a sounder and more properly functioning body. What have I gained if my money goes to treat my disease rather than to enhance my life and that of others? Where then is the prosperity? If I spend years working in a manner that abuses my body and my health and will shorten the duration and quality of my life, what have I prospered? If I over indulge in food and drink and never properly exercise and condition my body, how will my next big bonus check offset my diabetes or high blood pressure? It simply doesn't add up. True prosperity is in striking a happy medium that includes our work and proper attention and maintenance to our physical and mental health. For us to do otherwise is to simply make the hospitals and pharmaceutical companies wealthier and prove us to be not so wise. Working yourself sick only to have to pay that income out in medical costs is not a good equation for success.

By far the most valuable and coveted asset in our prosperity package lies in our relationships. It is through our relationships that we can find help, motivation and support. The richness of relationships gives purpose and meaning to all the other areas of our prosperity. The victories are sweeter, the setbacks less painful when we can share them with others. Our natural human tendency is to seek validation to our work and achievements. It is through relationships that we have witness to who we are and what we accomplish in this life. The Beatles shared these thought-provoking words in their song, "*Can't Buy Me Love:*"

"Tell me that you need the kind of things
That money just can't buy,
I don't care too much for money
Money can't buy me love."

Howard Hughes was one of the wealthiest and most creative men in the world. As his life unfolded, he chose an eccentric and reclusive lifestyle that pulled him deeper within an existence of depression and pain. Meaningful relationships with family or friends faded into his memories. Although rich in dollars, he lived a life of self-imposed incarceration as he failed to realize the life-giving power and energy of meaningful relationships. Hughes succumbed to ill health at the age of seventy. His demise was brought on from his lack of physical care and the effects of medications for pain and other issues related to his severe obsessive-compulsive disorder.

Money could not buy Howard Hughes happiness, true friends or love. He obtained many creative goals. He made a great deal of money, but dd he truly live a life filled with prosperity? Did he learn and experience that the true treasures in life are only those that flow to us from our relationships and willingness to engage with the people in our lives who we value the most? The best feeling and greatest exhilaration in our life is to realize that we are valuable to someone else in this world.

The final puzzle piece of our prosperity resides in the achievement of our goals and ambitions in life. The pride and feeling of accomplishment in setting and reaching goals is an adrenaline rush that is hard to beat. The injection of energy to our self worth, our self confidence and our willingness to try even harder, are unmatched. Money alone cannot replace the sheer joy of accomplishment, even though they often come hand in hand. Our prosperity consciousness is grounded deep in our thoughts and visions of what we wish to achieve and accomplish.

Every achievement is born from a dream or thought. That thought is then spoken and written down. We then take action and work to make our visions manifest into reality. Accomplishment and achievement are an integral part of what determines our prosperity. We may not achieve every dream, but it shouldn't keep us from trying. We build a bridge in our lives to abundance through our recognition and homage to the prosperity in the universe. We seek to share that abundance with others, for it is the sharing that is the indicator of caring. As Mick Jaggar of the Rolling Stones stated, *"Life is a constant negotiation between our desires and our necessities."* As the lyrics to their song, *"You Can't Always Get What You Want,"* indicates,

*"You can't always get what you want,
But if you try sometimes,
Well you just might find you get what you need."*

Living in true prosperity means that you must approach life with a prosperity consciousness. You must embrace the *"glass is half full"* mentality and approach to life. Our thoughts determine our actions and our actions determine our reality. If we slide into a consciousness of lack and scarcity, then that is what will manifest itself in our lives. There is a great metaphysical principle that states, *"Thoughts held in mind produce after their kind."* Since science tells us that matter is neither create nor destroyed, only changed in form, we must then assume that the abundance of the world and the universe are constantly at our disposal. It is up to us to tap into the abundance of life and claim it for ourselves and to share the excess that flows to us with the rest of God's creations.

We must train our thoughts to visualize prosperity. We must pray and meditate on the fullness of the earth and God's universe. We must express gratitude for our blessings today and those that are on the way to our future. It is gratitude and thanksgiving that opens the door to the infinite abundance of our future. Gratitude entices us to give of our time, talents and treasures. We put ourselves into the divine flow of the universe and share the abundance while enjoying the never-ending stream of prosperity in our lives. No matter how hard we may try, we simply can't out give God.

So, then what is the secret to living a life of prosperity? Where and how do we develop a true prosperity consciousness in a world that provides the daily mirage of lack? It must start in our recognition that we live in a world and universe that is centered on abundance. Lack is fiction perpetrated by those who do not embrace the creative nature of the universe. We must train our minds and our hearts to live a daily routine that brings forth gratitude and inspires us to share our time, talent and money with others. Each morning, I pray the simplest yet most direct of prayers when I say, *"Thank you God."* If you seek one daily and concise message to relay to the creator, then let those words of gratitude be your choice.

My prayer and goal each day is to go out into the world and make a positive and profound difference in the lives of others. I seek to sow the seeds of happiness, peace, abundance and love. I grow rich through sharing my prosperity, not by hoarding it. If my light is to shine in this world, I cannot hide in under a bushel as the Bible states. Prosperity and abundance are meant to be shared. In athletics, we strive to win the championship trophy. It is the symbolic idol that is reflective of our success. As our personal life light dims and flickers out, we will not be revered and remembered in the moments after we are gone by how much money we gave or how many trophies we won. Our lasting and impactful legacy will be rooted in how much we gave of ourselves to others. That is the truth and the magic of true prosperity.

Lesson Ten

Champions Are Created by Those Who Finish Second

> *"You cannot eliminate a champion of the heart by numbers on a scoreboard. Their heart, spirit and soul do not have to adorn a first-place medal to display their love, respect and compassion for others."*
>
> ***Fred Clausen***

Every champion was created and made stronger in that quest by the challenge of those who finished second. The competitive nature can be a double-edged sword. Without the motivational push from the competition to keep us focused and dedicated to improving our team and ourselves, we would never reach the pinnacle of the champion. Why then do we tend to shove those who have helped to hone us into the disdain and obscurity that has been associated with coming in second? Great value lies in knowing that our competition will be skillful, dedicated and motivated as well. It is this acute psychological trigger that is the impetus for us to work harder, prepare in more detail and perform at a higher level when the games begin.

Those who finished second have demanded the best from the champion in their quest to claim the prize. At times, it is in being second that we realize, in various aspects of our skills and preparation; we are on the very cusp of greatness. The silver medal gages how close we are to total success if we only work a little harder, longer and more focused. Being second is no disgrace nor is it indicative of branding someone a loser. After all, to be second you must have left all competitors save one in your dust. There is always honor in giving your best.

Forty years of coaching and athletic administration taught me many things about life and people. I have already shared a few. I have seen and experienced the hours upon hours of hard work and dedication of my athletes and my fellow coaches as we reached together for the stars. I have shouted with joy at victory and wept in disappointment at defeat. One of the main things I learned in all those years that stood head above my other lessons is, there are many championship-class people who never finish first. I learned that being first in my life isn't nearly as important as the lessons I learned and being a kind and caring person. I can embrace the heart and spirit of a champion without having to physically hoist the trophy.

If you will indulge me, I am going to provide some viable insights on how being second can provide us the needed strength and motivation to take us to a higher plain of thought and an even greater elevation of our humanness. At the same time, I seek to show how a mentality of *"others first"* can change our thoughts, actions and the results in our lives as well. I have watched throughout my life as the respect and the manners of each generation have eroded away. Being a kind and loving person involves the admiration and respect for others that allows our ego to step back and let someone else be first. You don't have to lose yourself, or any preconceived notion of gain to have manners and put others first. In the competition of life, we don't have to beat all others to enjoy the accolades of a wonderful, enjoyable and fruitful existence. I maximize my personal human potential by being the best *"me"* that I can possibly be. Where I rank in the standings matters little in relationship to where I rank in doing my very best in all areas of my life.

So many people will push and shove their way to be first in line, first to enter a door or first to run you over on the highway in their efforts to be first to wherever it is they are going. I believe that our innate human drive to be first can be obsessive to the point that it is potentially one of the most damaging and detrimental characteristics to our personal and spiritual growth and development. How can you teach someone to share as a child when you don't model that behavior? How can you cut in line at the store or push your way to the front of the concert entry and still profess to teach and practice caring for others and good manners? Why do some people consciously and habitually open doors so that others may pass first, while others slam the door in your face in an unconscious move of self-centeredness?

The famous actor and dancer Fred Astaire once said, *"The hardest job kids have today is learning good manners without seeing any."* Emily Post added, *"Manners are a sensitive awareness of the feelings of others. If you have that awareness, you have good manners, no matter which fork you use."* The act of displaying respect and good manners is as simple as making a few small sacrifices that provide others the opportunity to know you care. In today's world, it is almost stunning to see a gentleman open a door for a lady or see them pull out her chair to seat her.

Equal rights for women did not mean they forfeited the right for one to show respect and kindness in the form of good manners. I open doors for my wife, but I also open doors for friends and even strangers, men and women. I can be a champion in spreading a little respect, joy and even awe by sacrificing being first to slip into a room or line of traffic. In some things in my life I am happy and self gratified to come in second. The *"me first"* mantra of many in the world today is driving a wedge between us and our relationships. *"Me first":* a philosophy and associated conduct that when left unchecked can lead to uncontrolled anger, aggression, bullying, road rage and raise one's stress level through the roof. How do some fail to comprehend that respect and kindness lead to peace and contentment?

Let's circle back to my athletic career for a moment. YES! I have always played and coached to win. I have also always sought to be the type of person who is kind, considerate and polite. Being second requires a great deal of personal humility and introspection. Like everyone else, I want to be first. I want to win. I want to be the best. I take tremendous pride in giving total dedication and effort to anything I undertake, as should we all. I have become wise enough to know there is more to be learned from competition than just hoisting the trophy. What good are our life experiences if we don't learn, grow and become better in some manner?

I am continually amazed at the stigma we sometimes attach to those who finish second in a game, in a race, in any endeavor to which they have poured their effort, heart and soul. How can we not realize that except for one bounce of the ball, or one flip of the coin, the order of finish could have easily been changed? How can we walk through life each day not giving respect and encouragement to our fellow man with a kind word or gesture to allow them in the moment to be first? Are we sometimes so blinded to the sensitive nature of our interactions with others that we tend to ignore or not even acknowledge their existence and relevance?

My scouting is a bit different now than it was when I was coaching. Instead of charting the opponents, I choose to look for, identify and honor the everyday champions in my world. These are common people who do extraordinary acts of kindness asking nothing in return. Several months ago, I was in the dollar store waiting in line to pay for my selections. A young man and his girlfriend were in line in front of me. They had a basket load of items and I could tell that they were quickly trying to do the math to make sure that they had the funds to pay the bill. In front of them was an elderly lady who seemed to be wrestling with her goods as the clerk checked her out and bagged her items. She walked with a cane which left her no margin for error in trying to balance her purchases. As she struggled and juggled for a moment, she dropped one of her bags. Without hesitation, the young man sprang forward and not only picked up the dropped items, but insisted that he help her to her car. He reassured his girlfriend that he would be right back as the cashier was now ringing up their items. The look of gratitude and relief on the elderly lady's face was priceless. Simple, spontaneous, unselfish acts of putting someone else first, lights the lamp of love in the universe.

The kindness and thoughtfulness of the young man was heartwarming. I couldn't help myself. As the young man returned I looked this total stranger in the eyes and told him how proud I was of his decision to place someone else first. He was humble and almost a bit embarrassed by my acknowledgement of his gesture. I was so touched in fact that I asked, no insisted, that they allow me to pay for their items as a token of gratitude. This young couple got it. In a simple gesture of kindness, they exhibited the lessons of universal love that many seek years to master. You don't have to be first to be a winner…a champion. Putting others first is not a sacrifice. It is an opportunity for greatness of the heart and soul.

How often in our lives do we simply judge others by their performance in a manner that gives no honor to their total body of work? Maybe we should consider that in finishing second, or in just showing up in the world each day, we have bested many others. We often learn more about heart and perseverance from those who finish second than the winner themselves. A second-place finisher will often provide a more diligent and unique approach to new competition in the future in an effort to improve and fine tune their skills. Great innovations have come from second-place finishers who sought new and better ways to compete in any of life's endeavors.

Please don't misunderstand my intentions. I am not advocating that we work to finish second best, or even consider ourselves second rate at anything. What I do promote is that we allow others the courtesy to be first in our lives--in the lunch line, going in the door or pulling out in traffic. I advocate that we offer the respect and dignity of all of those who compete in life on a daily basis. There are times to rue being second place and there are times in which it is the kind and polite thing to do. If we are constantly pushing our way through life to always be first at the expense or exclusion of others, it can lead to damaging situations that can endanger our health, our peace of mind and our relationships.

A weak and shallow person often mistakes the sharp rudeness of their tongue and judgmental attitude to be an exhibition of strength and dominance. In reality, it is in fact reflective of mental and spiritual immaturity. Dave Willis, American author and actor encourages us to *"Show respect even to people who don't deserve it; not as a reflection of their character, but as a reflection of yours."* How do you allow others to show up in your world? When you walk in to the coffee shop tomorrow, will you invite that laborer scurrying to get to his painting job to move ahead of you in line? Will you smile and acknowledge strangers with a warm salutation?

Being kind to others is not a sign of weakness, but rather compassion. Honoring others with respect and courtesy are the indelible marks of a person who values his fellow man. When we show respect for others we are also showing respect for ourselves. We honor God and the universal energy of love when we, *"Do unto others, as we would have them do unto us."* The core values of being a champion run deeper than the scores, the wins, the trophies or the medals. A champion of the heart, mind and soul looks within for strength in all areas of themselves. You cannot eliminate a champion of the heart by the numbers on a scoreboard. A champion of the heart, spirit and soul does not have to adorn a first-place medal to display their love, respect and compassion for others.

I see champions each and every day in the people who cross my path in life. I see those who have every opportunity to quit, to complain, to be disrespectful and rude rise above that temptation and light up the day with a smile. I see their kindness rise above anger. I see their patience overcoming a world of frustrations. Do I not owe those champions the recognition and opportunity to be first in my small acknowledgment of their efforts? Kindness is contagious. My hope is that my lead in being *"second"* to honor the rest of mankind at times sparks others to open the door of love and respect in their daily interactions and relationships. In my athletic career, I was determined to never be outworked or out hustled by the competition. As I walk through life today, far removed from that competitive arena, my prayer and goal each day is to be a blessing and a difference maker in the lives of those whose eyes meet mine and whose path I intersect. I will joyfully defer to being *"second"* in their honor.

Lesson Eleven

The Clock of Life Has No Timeouts

> *"Time has many ways of exhibiting its value in our life. Often the greatest gift that we receive is that of someone's personal time shared with us. Providing our own time to someone else is a divine gesture of love and concern."*
>
> *Fred Clausen*

Time is the one thing that we have a finite quantity of in life and in sports. In the 2009 Big 12 Conference Championship football game, the Texas Longhorns trailed the Nebraska Cornhuskers by two points with only a few seconds left in the game. Texas was out of time outs and needed to get the field goal team on the field to make an attempt for the game winning kick. On the play immediately prior to place kicker Hunter Lawrence's field goal attempt, as the game clock ticked down, Texas quarterback Colt McCoy rolled far to the right with Nebraska's star defensive tackle Ndamukong Suh in hot pursuit. McCoy fired a pass well downfield and out of bounds as time expired. As all zeros flashed across the scoreboard clock it appeared that time had run out, which would have ended the game with Nebraska winning 12–10.

Not so fast, my Cornhusker friends! Pursuant to NCAA rules, the video replay official determined that an *"egregious"*, and therefore reviewable, error concerning the game clock had occurred. The officials ordered the errantly elapsed one second be returned to the clock. The ESPN/ABC video feed showed that McCoy's pass had hit a stadium railing out of bounds with: 01 left, allowing Texas to kick the winning field goal to advance to the BCS title game. Time...precious time! My wife and I happened to be personal witnesses, in AT&T Stadium that December evening, to this miraculous use of one single second to turn the entire results of a championship game.

Time is an elusive variable in every event in our lives. Only in sports can we put time back on the clock or add seconds to the length of a contest. Life does not afford us that luxury. As time slips away, it is never to be recovered. Life doesn't provide us the time and opportunity for a *"do over"*, an opportunity to play the scene again. It will however, often allow us an opportunity for a *"redo"* in which we can make adjustments and hopefully embrace a more productive outcome or a similar action. Simply stated, the exact moment in time can never be replayed, but we can use the precious moments ahead to alter the direction and success in our lives if we consciously make meaningful changes in a timely manner.

I'm sure, at some point, we have all uttered the phrase, *"I had the time of my life."* Have you ever really analyzed that statement as it actually relates to time and timing in our existence? We could extract a literal meaning from this simple phrase and interpret it to mean that out of all of our many seconds, minutes, hours and days, these moments were the very best, the most impactful, the most memorable. My personal perception of time often mirrors the image brought to mind in the lyrical chorus of the Steve Miller Band song, *"Fly Like an Eagle:"*

> *"Time keeps on slippin', slippin', slippin'*
> *Into the future"*

Time is our greatest, yet most undervalued asset. The timing in life and our time management can be revealed as one of our most coveted allies or it can manifest as our worst enemy. We sprint through our youth thinking we have unlimited days, months and years for our lives to unfold. We squander opportunities and moments in time through our blind push to hurry the world along with our wildly impatient indifference. So many things in life we want right now in a manifestation of instant gratification. I can plead guilty to that in my gardening habits. My wife and friends know me as the guy who expects spring to last about three hours in my back yard as I transition the area from winter to a lush and flowering tropical summer. I buy larger and blooming plants to give me the *"wow"* right now. Each of us seeks to manipulate time and situations to suit our own agenda. We often are not mentally and spiritually disciplined enough to allow God and the universe to present the right and perfect gifts to us at the right and perfect time. Like my gardening, we want the payoff immediately, if not sooner.

Mother Teresa's guiding words tell us, *"You may not understand today or tomorrow, but eventually God will reveal why you went through everything that you did."* We seek to exert control on our life clock and to make the world turn on our schedule. We blindly push ahead with little or no regard for all of the universal things which must be aligned for our well being and success. When our world turns upside down we often seek answers through our tears as to *"why me?"* and *"why now?"* Time is not ours to manipulate. There are two things in life that money can never buy us: true love and more time. Ironically, our true happiness and success are highly dependent on how and with whom we spend our time. We must choose wisely and manage prudently.

There are many skills in sports and in life, which require us to perfect our timing. We also must develop an approach of patience to allow things to materialize or align to serve us in the best way possible. The skill of bringing our timely swing, throw or other actions into play at the precise moment that will provide the greatest opportunity for success, takes patience and persistence. A fraction of a second off can determine the difference between success and failure.

Each day we hinge our lives on the timing of certain vital and important things. Timing is being in the right position at the right time and performing the correct action. Often, we must exercise extreme patience and persistence, which allows us to execute a timely maneuver, whether in sports or in life, that will have a meaningful impact on our direction and success. Time is the duration or precise instant that something happens. The question that I pose is, does time align simultaneously in the entire universe at one moment? If I am in New York, the *"moment"* in the universe is the same as in London, in Tokyo, or Moscow but the time on the clock is decidedly different. So how do I actually gage time in my life? Do I record the *"moments"* in time or the numbers in hours on the clock in my relationship with time? Or is that distinction even relevant?

In baseball, the hitter is striving to time the pitch to swing and make contact at just the right and perfect angle and bat speed. The pitcher on the other hand, is working to disrupt the timing of the hitter by changing the speed and location of his pitches. Setting our mind to hit a 95 mile-per-hour fastball can be greatly interrupted if an 80 mile-per-hour curveball floats into the strike zone. Our lives mirror that same need to recognize and adjust our timing. We lunge and swat with the greatest of intentions, but the worst of timing in life when the speed and direction of things around us seek to disrupt our performance through distraction. Many factors seek to disrupt the timing in our lives. We must stay focused to succeed. We must also live each day in the *"here and now"* as we strive to avoid the deceptions of our past and the romantic lure of our future. This day, this hour, this moment is all that we can count on.

Life often requires us to bob and weave through the day and adjust our rate of acceleration in engaging the world. A running back in football must learn how to seemingly drift behind his blockers with a patient anticipation and timing until a seam opens up and he explodes through into the secondary. Investment brokers will tell you that the two things necessary for success in the markets is timing and the patience to ride the fluctuating daily highs and lows. Millions are gained and lost by timely market decisions and actions. Good timing will only pay dividends if we have the patience to allow the pieces to fall into their intended places before we burst through into greatness.

By no means is patience easy to master. Let's examine for a moment what I like to refer to as the *"Santa Clause"* perception of time. This is my purely unscientific perception of how time passes when we stare at the clock in our best Jedi impression of trying to speed it up or slow it down. Remember the excitement and even nervousness that you felt as a child every Christmas Eve? The anticipation of what was to come sparked an anxiety level that kept us awake while we watched the clock and listened for auditory evidence that Santa had made his appearance. The seconds, minutes and hours seemed to drag by in snail-like fashion while our eagerness to engage the joys of Christmas Day ran amuck in our minds. Try as we might, sleep usually overtook our efforts to speed up the clock. Suffice it to say that, as children, we literally wanted time and Santa to fly.

Oh, how our perception and wishes change as we age and hopefully grow wiser. As the years of our lives tick away, we reach that moment when it suddenly strikes us that we are like the baseball player caught off guard in trying to adjust our timing and hit the curveball. Adjusting to the steady shift and reality of our time suddenly is of the greatest importance. We gaze into the mirror one day to find a face that more closely resembles our parents than the youthful self-image we carry in our minds.

Time has many ways of exhibiting its value in our life. Often the greatest gift we receive is that of someone's personal time shared with us. Providing our own time to someone else is a divine gesture of love and concern. You have heard it said that we must live in the moment, for once that moment is gone we can never get it back again. There is no time like the present because the present time is all that we really have available to us. Yesterday is gone and only a memory. Tomorrow is never guaranteed. Each of us longs for time with a loved one who has transitioned. Our dreams allow us to be time travelers, if only for awhile to move back and forth into our alter reality and times either past or future.

If you have read my writings thus far, you have most likely surmised that I am a big fan of Yogi Berra and his *"Yogism"* quotes. The thing about Yogi's quotes is that if you think about them aside from their humor, many have a profound message in reality. I know…scary! When asked about the shadows in left field at Yankee stadium in the early fall afternoons, Yogi provided a whimsical, *"It gets late early out here."* A profound and yet contradictory thought all in one. However, to me it is what I assert to be the perfect observation in my own life when it turns dark in December at 5:30 p.m. in the evening.

To expose yet another layer of Yogi's insight, I have also pondered the meaning to be that our life can skirt by in a blur if we don't engage in and live in the moment. All too early in life, the eclipsing darkness will be upon us. We all know people who have allowed it to get late way too early in their lives. They quit living and engaging by sitting on the sidelines or riding their own psychological time machine either into their past or what they have projected as their future. I caution again that now, the present moment, is all that we are guaranteed. As Robin Williams' character John Keating shared in the 1989 movie *Dead Poets Society*, "*Carpe Diem. Seize the day Boys. Make your life extraordinary.*" Make the most of your present moments.

The Nobel Prize winning scientist Albert Einstein emphasized that, *"Time is an illusion."* Einstein believed that the past, the present and the future coexist in time. He also acknowledged that the perception of time is determined by the position and state of mind of the observer. I often had that feeling as I have traveled the world myself. If I am in Australia and it is sixteen clock hours ahead of the time in my home in Texas, does that mean I am living the future of the reality of the time that will be in Texas? Or am I possibly living out three hours later than the time that has already passed on the International Date Line? Time is relative to our position. Without getting into the science of time and relativity, and I am certainly no Einstein, I think that it is fair and just to say that our personal perception of time is greatly dependent on our view and position of life and the world.

So time and timing are the great variable in our lives. There are so many things that we might have done if the clock hadn't run out or if our timing had been better. So much of life is time sensitive. The rock band Chicago left us to wonder with their lyrics,

"Does anybody really know what time it is?
Does anybody really care?"

Time awareness becomes keener with age. Time is a commodity that meant very little to me in my younger years but has become priceless to me as I age. We all think we are bullet proof and will live forever when we are young, and then we slip into the reality that life offers us a finite number of seconds, and that exact number is an unknown. The great juggling act of our lives is to use our time wisely and to also manage our time and lives with a patient and persistent prudence and respect. Time lost or squandered can never be regained.

Our ongoing battle with father time requires a large dose of both patience and persistence. To paraphrase an old saying, *"Patience allows us the time for our life to fall into place."* Patience is the unfolding and demonstration of the conscious wisdom that we understand that certain things take time and divine order to unfold and manifest in our lives. Persistence is our willingness to not be discouraged nor deterred as we patiently work towards our goals. Our persistent mindset in the timely pursuit of our dreams and goals insures that our prudent use of time and effort has not been wasted.

In the words of Paramahansa Yogananda, *"Persistence guarantees that results are inevitable."* Persistence does not mean that you won't have trials and failures. It means that you will valiantly continue time after time to try again. Persistence is our ability and determination to press on in the face of adversity. It is the attitude and strength of will that no matter how many times I get knocked down, I will get up and get back into the game--into my pursuit of victory.

Napoleon Hill, the renowned author of *Think and Grow Rich* stated, *"Patience, persistence and perspiration make an unbeatable combination for success."* The message that I have gleaned over the years from these knowledgeable masters, thinkers and writers is that we must use our time wisely and judiciously and also understand that in this pursuit we must have an understanding that it will not necessarily happen on our schedule. The Bible tells us in Ecclesiastes 3:1, *"To everything there is a season, and a time to every purpose under heaven."* Our challenge is to persistently prepare, work towards and be patient for that time to come. Every time we fail and rise to try again, we are one step closer to success.

Lesson Twelve

Harness the Creative Power of Your Imagination

> *"A dream that arises from our creative imagination, remains just a dream until we attach it to an action plan for creation. Dreams without action will remain only dreams—aloof and incomplete."*
>
> *Fred Clausen*

The master of imagination, Dr. Seuss, cleverly challenged us to, *"Think left and think right and think low and think high. Oh, the thinks you can think up if only you try!"* Of all the magic that transcends our senses and conscious world, our imagination bids us to travel to scenes never experienced—to create our tomorrows—to touch our future—to live our dreams. When we look out across the ocean, sort images in the clouds, or close our eyes to witness an alter reality, we are using the most powerful tool in our creative mind. It has been the imaginative genius of those who have come before us that has created the world that we revel in today. Henry David Thoreau shared with us, *"This world is but a canvas for our imagination."* Within our mind resides the creative power of imagination that has served to give birth to every invention, and achievement known to man.

Albert Einstein wrote, *"Imagination is more powerful than knowledge. For knowledge is limited to all we know and understand, while imagination embraces the entire world, and all there will ever be to know and understand."* The imagination is limitless in its ability to allow us both freedom and power. Nothing has ever been created or achieved in life without it first being a burning image in our mind's eye. It is that spark that stirs the emotion and creative urge within us all. To limit our imagination is to limit our scope of understanding, and thus impede our relationships to the world, to God and to the universe. It is through our imagination that we form a connecting bond to the divine energy of God. A dream that comes true, or our imagination brought to life, is a tribute to the creative energy of the universe. Is it not quite feasible that our imaginations are the whispers and images of God's creative plan?

Helen Keller once said, *"The most beautiful world is always entered through imagination."* Though born blind and deaf, Helen Keller's mind and imagination had to have been powerfully strong to create the reality of her world. Her imaginative world had to become her world of reality as well. She stretched her imagination to overcome the absence of two of her most creative senses. All of us have the inherent seeds of a vivid imagination and a creative intellect. It is how we choose to use our imagination and transfer those images in our collective thoughts into our physical world that can be magical. An author puts pen to paper. An artist puts brush to canvas. A sculptor chisels out the image trapped in the stone. It is when we take the images of our imagination, and combine them with our skillful creative action, that our dreams become a reality.

Eleanor Roosevelt stated, *"The greatest gift that we can give to a child is imagination."* Imagination, at any age, is the freest form of our childhood. As children, we often let our imaginations lead us on magical journeys and experiences, as we sought to construct a competing universe in our thoughts. We met imaginary friends. We had imaginary pets. We lived in imaginary places of beauty and grandeur as we created blueprints of elaborate castles in our mind. We promoted ourselves to become a princess or a star athlete who headlined the show each and every day. We dreamed as dreamers should. Imagination gives us hope, courage and joy. It allows us to escape the present in our efforts to create a better and more beautiful, more loving future.

Some people are labeled as *"dreamers"* in life. The usual inference is that these souls reside more in the imaginative world than in the world of reality. For some individuals, this may have basis in fact. However, I counter that perception to say that if it were not for the *"dreamers,"* our world, our lives, would never have risen to the advanced realities of our modern era. It is our dreams that give our imagination purpose. Our dreams show us what we want—

what is possible. Imagination provides us with a creative link to the divine spirit that resides within us. Our imagination provides us with a host of ways that we might realize those dreams. A dream that arises from our creative imagination remains just a dream until we attach it to an action plan for creation.

Imagination fosters visionary thinking beyond the scope of our sense of sight. These visionary thoughts give rise to constructive action and great achievements. Dreams often come upon us in our sleep in a random array and with no logical meaning. Imagination allows us to construct targeted dreams of our own creation. One notable example was the collective dreams of the 1980 United States Ice Hockey team. A group of young and energetic United States college hockey players took the ice in the Winter Olympics in Lake Placid, New York that winter against a rugged and seasoned team from the Soviet Union. The Soviets had won the Olympic Gold medal in men's hockey for six consecutive Winter Olympiads. No one in the world gave the United States team a chance to win--No one had the creative imagination to believe that this inexperienced group of young kids could win this medal round encounter--No one that is, except for those twenty players and their coach, Herb Brooks.

It is in the collective energy of our imagination that our goals and our destiny can come together, if only for a brief moment in time. This is precisely what occurred in 1980 on the ice in Lake Placid. The United States hockey team battled from behind to win the game 4-3 and go on to win the Olympic Gold medal by defeating Finland in the finals. The United States victory over the Soviets became known as the *"Miracle on Ice."* In 1999, *Sports Illustrated* magazine declared the upset as the top sports moment of the 20th century. Before we can achieve something, we must first create it in our imagination—our reflective thoughts—our vision. The imagination and dreams of those young men united and solidified on the ice in Lake Placid that night to produce a moment now frozen in time.

Our dreams and our accomplishments take early root in our imagination. It is our willingness to dream and, to also work to make those dreams come true, that will bring them to fruition. Dreams without action will remain only dreams—aloof and incomplete. As the late-great boxer Muhammad Ali shared, *"The man who has no imagination has no wings."* When we gain our imaginative wings, we ignite our passion and create our own future. Our imagination stimulates our creativity and sparks our intellect and innovation. Even as we grow older, our imagination brings a sense of magic and possibility into our lives in a world where reality often disappoints. It is in the deep recesses of our imagination that our visions form and come into focus.

The experiences of life have a way of dulling our imagination. Where in our young lives does our imagination begin to fade and our creativity become stifled? Why do we allow others in our lives to dictate to us what to dream and how to create it? Why do we accept someone else's evaluation of what is possible for us to achieve? Why do we often seek security within the tangible world, rather than reaching into our own imagination and crafting a better, more loving and peaceful one? The guardianship of the imagination resides within each of us individually. We alone control the filter to our thoughts and the gateway to our imagination. Actor Gene Wilder expressed quite eloquently the mystique of our *"Pure Imagination,"* in the song by the same name in the famous movie, Willy Wonka and the Chocolate Factory:

"Come with me and we'll be in a world of pure imagination. There is no life that I know to compare with pure imagination. Living there, you'll be free if you truly wish to be."

The thought provoking and mental stimulation from music, movies, books, art, nature, and our spiritual awareness, serves to fuel our pure imagination daily. Our creative imagination allows us to transition from playing with toy cars as a child to designing them as an adult. We move from whimsical dreams and thoughts of physical prowess to achievement in any competitive arena that we choose. According to Albert Einstein, *"Imagination is everything. It is the preview of life's coming attractions."* We are the architects of our past, present and future realities. Our imagination is often anchored in the faith that we embrace in the source of our thoughts. I choose to believe that my imagination and creative thoughts are divinely inspired as part of God's creative plan. We are partners with the divine energy in co-creating our world. I often ponder what the biblical character Noah must have imagined when given instructions by God to build a huge ark on dry land. That architectural masterpiece took both divine inspiration and Noah's vivid imagination to assemble. It also took a great deal of faith in the source of the inspiration.

As productive as our imaginative thoughts can be, there are many times in our lives that we unconsciously create an overactive imagination. This is especially true in regard to fear. Our imagination can serve us well. However, if left to run amuck, it can stifle our energy and our actions and leave us in mental and emotional paralysis. As expressed by the singing group The Temptations in one of their famous songs, our fear and anxiety is often, *"Just my imagination, running away with me."* As we strive to approach life from a positive and optimistic plane, we learn to control our imagination and those silent whispers of doubt that can plague our progress. Experience teaches us that most of the monsters born in our imagination have no foundation in truth and reality. At times, it seems that we all have walked that fine line between the truth of our creative imagination and the darkness of debilitating psychosis. As vivid as our thoughts might be at times, it is vital for us not to lose ourselves in a maze beyond the scope of reality.

Our imagination can also lead us into a deeper relationship and understanding of ourselves and the world around us. My games of imagination have changed over the course of my life. I once centered my imaginative powers on those budding visions of youthful folly. I dreamed many dreams and imagined many roads to a life of success, glamour, and wealth. Many of my dreams fell by the wayside while others blossomed and became even more than I could have imagined. You see, imagination and dreaming are a numbers game. Our imagination is not finite, and it gives us many opportunities to dream a new dream if one slips away. All our dreams and imaginative ideas will not come to pass. The masters of imagination and creative genius in life are those who learn to dream that new and bigger dream. For a dreamer, failure is not an ending, but the beginning of a new opportunity to fine tune, retool and put our creative imagination back to work.

My days are now filled with a different type of imagination. I watch people everywhere that I go—in all situations—in all walks of life. I observe how they interact with the world and how they embrace life. I use my imagination to place myself, at least mentally, in the shoes of that particular person. I wonder what their life must be like. I imagine the road they might have traveled to their place in life today. I let my imagination create within my mind a million more reasons to be thankful—to feel blessed. I imagine ways in which I can become a personal blessing to others and a voice of peace, love and understanding in a chaotic world. The same magic and powerful imagination that fired my soul as a young man, now fuels my desire to be a servant leader.

I have learned the difference between my creative imagination and the illusions and mirages that often cloud our minds. I still dream, and I still seek to create. I imagine new ideas and actions each day that I can manifest to bring a little more love and joy into my life and into the lives of those with whom I will interact. I dream of creating and improving relationships with my family and friends. The wealth that I imagine now lies in creating a prosperity consciousness laden with peace and love. I imagine being able to be a positive influence in the lives of those people in my life who need a kind word, a gentle touch and steadfast friend. I imagine my words and deeds becoming a motivation and an inspiration to solicit other dreamers to look into the world and ignite their own creative forces.

If we only leave one legacy in our life, let it be that we used our imagination and creative energy to give vision to our own dreams and to those of others. Let us seek to teach and encourage those who share their dreams with us. Let us nurture our spirit to be open to the infinite possibilities of love within the universe. We must never underestimate the power of our creative imagination and our ability to shift the tides of meaningful change in the world. Mother Teresa dreamed of a world free of hunger, pain and disease. She put her imagination into action as an agent of love and comfort for those who had no voice in the world. She lifted the hopes and dreams of many downtrodden souls and gave vision and motivation to countless others. Her simple words serve as a divinely inspired reminder, *"I alone cannot change the world, but I can cast a stone across the waters to create many ripples."* It is our challenge to let our imaginations create the ripples of love, peace, and change that can raise the tides of awareness. Imagine what we can accomplish if we all seek to co-create from the divine energy of love.

Lesson Thirteen

Condition Your Body to Improve Your Game and Your Life

> *"A day of healthy living is priceless.*
> *A day which allows us to experience and relish the activities and people that bring us joy, love and pleasure is beyond measure."*
>
> **Fred Clausen**

In 1970 I was a nineteen-year-old freshman playing baseball on a scholarship at St. Mary's University in San Antonio, Texas. My weight and body had ballooned up to two hundred and twenty-five pounds from the svelte one ninety-five that I weighed in my senior year in high school. We're not talking muscle here either. I guess the *"freshman fifteen"* for weight gained the first year in college applied to guys as well. Needless to say, I found myself sitting in the head coach's office having been summoned there for a heart-to-heart discussion about my expanded state of affairs. The message provided to me that day was simple: lose twenty-five pounds or lose your scholarship. The lifelong message was made clearer as well. Conditioning your body was not only healthier, but vital to performance and even your state of finances.

With a great deal of newly inspired self discipline and a lot of time on the jogging track and in the weight room, I was able to learn that pushing away from the meal and snack table was the exercise I needed the most. Thus, began my lifelong saga of the battle of the bulge. I lost the twenty-five pounds, retained my scholarship and found that my body felt better and operated much more efficiently when I was in shape and fit. What a novel concept! As simple as it may seem, millions of us around the world let our eating habits and lack of proper exercise put us in a health-risk situation that can literally cost us hundreds of thousands of dollars in our lifetimes, as well as our lives themselves.

Josh Billings, nineteenth century humorist, writer and lecturer wrote, *"Health is like money, we never have a true idea of its value until we lose it."* I would like to say that over the years, I have retained the discipline and dietary habits to remain the lean mean fighting machine that I was in my college years. That is simply not true. I have had a constant love affair with everything sugar and fried that has kept me on a physical yoyo and the weight scale watch list. More times than not, after reaching the tipping point of tipping the scales, I have battled back to regain my health and fitness. I also regained an opportunity to change my eating and exercise habits to a more moderate and sustainable level. Mahatma Gandhi hit the nail on the head in his quote, *"It is health that is real wealth and not gold or silver."*

Let's explore together why physical fitness and a healthy body can pay excessive dividends throughout your life. As a former high school biology and health teacher, I am keenly aware of the science behind a balanced diet accentuated with proper conditioning and strength training. As a former coach and athletic director, I am also well versed in the extended performance level of the body in the competitive arena. Your body, health and fitness level are a direct reflection of your lifestyle choices. If you choose to eat right and exercise, then your body will serve you well for many years regardless of most of your genetic predispositions. If you choose to overindulge in food and drink and lumber around in a sloth-like existence, your well-oiled machine of a body will more quickly than not turn into a broken-down mass of dysfunctional parts and betraying maladies.

I am certainly not into *"fat shaming,"* because I have throughout the years not set the best of examples. I do know a great deal about my own body when at times, I have let my weight and physical condition run amuck. For every ten pounds that I am overweight, that is an extra mile of blood vessels and capillaries that my heart has to pump through. My heart, which is designed to perform at a certain ideal body weight and work capacity will carry the extra load for a while but be put under undue stress which will most likely cut short its lifetime warranty. Add to that a family history of heart problems and high blood pressure and you are creating the perfect storm.

But wait, there's more. When my abdominal cavity begins to expand with inflated fat cells because my diet is over the top and off the charts, there is increased pressure on those nearby digestive organs, and my lungs as well, since the room to expand is taken up by the fat. I now have shorter breathing capacity, increased blood pressure, more stress on my joints from the extra weight and the distinct possibility of developing diabetes and other related ailments. Unchecked over time, we can and do simply eat our way to a reduced level of health and bodily function and most likely an earlier than necessary demise. We struggle to sleep due to acid reflux, and we stock our closets with a variety of clothing sizes to meet our particular season of expansion.

I most recently ate my way to a miserable and unhealthy two hundred and forty-three pounds. I have done this more than a few times in my life and have managed to fight my way back to a healthy condition and size 38 pants. So, as you can see, I am not the poster child for discipline in this area, especially as I have aged. I have rediscovered, yet again, the magic formula for maintaining a healthy body weight and fitness level: eat better and less--exercise more. Profound isn't it? The trick lies in having the mental discipline and accountability to get into a regular routine and to make it a lifestyle, not a diet and exercise program. I am personally back into a healthier existence after several months of working the plan. Now the hard part begins--sustaining.

My challenge, and that of many in staying healthy, is not in knowing what to do. The challenge is in finding and maintaining the discipline to do it and in a fashion and lifestyle which is sustainable. If you are lured into programs that are fast and furious and promise quick results, it will never be something which is sustainable over the course of your life. What if I told you that by walking a mile or two, four or five days a week and cutting your intake of junk food, you could lose a pound a week? Nobody ever advertises, *"Lose two pounds in two weeks,"* because it doesn't have flash and sex appeal. However, do you realize that by losing a pound a week over a year you can reduce your weight by fifty pounds? This gradual reduction in weight, and increase in fitness, will also lower your blood pressure and heart rate and increase your stamina. Doable and sustainable is a great motivator to long term health and fitness habits.

What I really want to emphasize in these words is not weight loss, healthy diet practices or fitness regiments. We've all been beaten over the head with those phrases. I want to make you aware that all these things are an integral part of living a happy and productive life. I want to walk through the extremely positive impacts that living healthier has on the distinct areas of your life which include your body function, the fun you have in life, the financial impact and your freedom. I also want to remind myself at the same time to constantly guard my greatest asset--my health. This journey begins by starting where we are now in the present moment, using what we have and doing what we can. We often have sacrificed our health and good habits in the pursuit of making a dollar in our youth. We miss meals, eat junk, forgo exercise and suffer from stress. Don't get me wrong, we all must make a living and provide for ourselves and our family. We must find a happy medium and give attention to our fitness as well. The consequences of a strategy that does not provide for that balance will trap us into paying dearly in our later years with poor health, possible limited mobility and the ever-increasing cost of health care that will milk our retirement funds dry.

I am going to make a confession. I have never been a big fan of math, even though I understand the importance it has to almost everything in our life. Once I cleared the hurdles of addition, subtraction, multiplication, division and fractions, I figured I had the tools I needed. Be that as it may, I was always intrigued by word problems. I have a math professor friend who I'm sure will tell me that once I enter the realm of word problems, then it becomes Algebra. Good health is a treasure at any stage in our lives. However, my aversion to Algebra aside, to illustrate the benefits of good health in your retirement years, let me present you with a simple word problem. I think the answer will be quite obvious even before you have to take out a pencil and paper.

Problem: Bob has retired with a million dollars in the bank and has an income of five thousand dollars per month. Jim also has a million dollars in the bank and also has a monthly income of five thousand dollars. Both Bob and Jim have the same amount of wealth.

Bob smoked all his life and is fifty pounds overweight. These issues require Bob to spend one thousand dollars per month or more on medications and doctor visits. He also pays premium prices for health insurance. Jim on the other hand never smoked, has maintained his fitness level, his weight and eats a balanced and healthy diet. Jim goes to the doctor once a year for a physical exam covered by his insurance and receives his well-patient shots and care as part of that. Jim's insurance premiums are lower than Bob's because he is a lower risk. Remember, both Bob and Jim have the same amount of wealth.

Question: Which of these two men has the greater amount of *disposable income?* The answer to the problem is rather obvious. More importantly, it is reflective of the costs associated with living a life of damaging health habits. Poor health is expensive and debilitating—especially as we age.

Although universal to all age groups and gender, I know young people who have allowed their obesity to dominate their health and take control of their capacity to live a normal and productive life. Their diminished health affects their personal life, their employment status and the associated economics. They relinquish control to food and drink while shunning the activities that can bring their bodies back into a healthier state. Happiness and the enjoyment of living an active, full life is a residual reward for taking care of yourself and your body. Surveys indicate that healthy people as a whole are happier, accomplish more personal goals and tend to exhibit a more positive approach to life.

Obviously, some health issues are born out of hereditary conditions, but many are self inflicted. Practicing good health, fitness and nutritional habits have even been shown to help overcome some of the genetic-related ailments. The ball is in our court.

Professional athletes and Olympic performers understand the need for fitness and a healthy training regiment and diet. They also make the connection between their fitness, their health and their ability to be successful and generate financial gain from their talents. The motivation may be slightly different for those of us in everyday life, but the opportunity for true gain in both finances and quality time are the same. A day of healthy living is priceless. A day which allows us to experience and relish the activities and people, who bring us joy, love and pleasure is beyond measure. It is no secret why some ninety-year-old senior adults still lead a healthy active and fun life. They discovered long ago the direct correlation between the discipline of exercise and proper nutrition and the active lifestyle they carry into their later years. They don't sit down and hope for the best. They engage and stay active which leads to a fuller more enjoyable existence. It's extremely difficult to climb the steps to the Acropolis in Athens, take a walk along the Great Wall of China or stroll around the Grand Canyon if you are using a walker.

It is vitally important to remember that the measure of our health also includes our mental health. Where our thoughts go, our energy will flow. What do you do on a daily basis to ensure that your thoughts are positive and productive? Are you a glass half full person or a glass half empty person? Do you quiet your mind as part of your exercise and relaxation routines through practices such as meditation? Do you read and practice the power of positive thinking? To exercise your body and ignore your mind is like the athlete who only lifts weights for their upper body while ignoring the power muscle groups in their legs, hips and back. A body out of balance will eventually run off the rails and have performance breakdowns and issues. Part of obtaining and maintaining good mental health is having outlets through which we can relieve stress. The worries of the world chase us around 24/7. It is vital to engage in both mental and physical activities that will provide the opportunity to relax and refresh.

Our brain is the most vital of our organs and the control center of all activities. A sound body still will not serve us well without a sharp and sound mind at the helm. It is the body's mainframe computer as well as the master of the chemical activities within. Our mental capacity requires constant exercise to remain sharp and attuned to the world around us. Those who continue a life that includes actively reading, working problems or crossword puzzles, engaging in meaningful discussions on current affairs, dabbling in creative adventures such as art or music and other mind-expanding play are less likely to develop memory related dysfunction as they age. The continuing message is that activity and exercise are the key components to remaining fit both physically and mentally. Buddha shared, *"To keep the body in good health is a duty...otherwise we shall not be able to keep our mind strong and clear."*

President Abraham Lincoln wisely stated, *"The best way to predict the future is to create it."* Each of us has charge of the care of our own bodies. The Bible instructs us in 1 Corinthians 6:19 that, *"Your body is a temple of the Holy Spirit within you."* I know what I need to do to be healthy and fit. I know how to do the things that will make me healthy and fit. As one of my coaches once told me, *"It's not the treadmills fault that you aren't losing weight if you never put yourself on it."* We are the architects of our future by the plans and actions that we execute today. If you are sixteen or sixty you can change your life for the better and improve your health, fitness and enjoyment of life starting today. Some things we have to do for ourselves in life. Others can cheer us on with support and motivation, but the toil and sweat must be our own to realize the benefits.

Lesson Fourteen

To Err is Human- To Forgive Sets Us Free

> *"Show me a person's attitudes and reactions to their mistakes and errors in life and I can provide you with a vivid portrait of their strength and character. Your heart can only be full of love if it has been filled by forgiveness and compassion."*
>
> **Fred Clausen**

I can safely say that none of us will live an error free life. At some point we all drop the ball, miss the goal or give into the situations and temptations that the human existence presents. In football when a defensive back makes a mistake, gets beat by the receiver and gives up a touchdown, the announcers will likely relate that the player needs to have a *"short memory"* in his next efforts. So, what the heck does that mean and how is it relevant to everyday life? The simplicity is that once a mistake is made, if we dwell on it, beat our self up psychologically, lose our focus and self confidence, then there is a very high likelihood that we will make another mistake to compound our situation in the very near future.

I love the wisdom and insight of the famous actor and martial arts master Bruce Lee when he shared, *"Mistakes are always forgivable, if one has the courage to admit them."* Perfection in life does not reside in being error free. We move closer to a more perfect existence when we master the ability to hold our self accountable for those mistakes. We bring our life more closely aligned with perfection when we use our mistakes and failures as learning experiences to broaden our insight and our resolve to do better. The first step as stated by Mr. Lee is admitting that we made a mistake or blew the assignment. By making that admission, we open our mind and spirit to adjusting our course and finding the positive and perfect solutions to our actions.

In righting our wrongs, realization is far more effective than rationalization. When my own children would occasionally get into trouble, I would hear every excuse in the world for why they did what they knew to be wrong. I'm pretty sure that we all have done the same. Rationalization is a fancy word for making excuses when we have no solid and valid answer for our actions. We seek to shift the blame or the impetus for the problematic behavior to something else or even someone else. We've all done it. It is human nature.

We learn that the only way to move forward fruitfully in life is to become smarter, stronger and more self-confident through the learning opportunities that our failures and missteps provide for us. The legendary college football coach from Alabama, Paul *"Bear"* Bryant had this to say, *"When you make a mistake, there are only three things that you should ever do about it; admit it, learn from it, and don't repeat it."* Our words of regret and admissions of being wrong and sorry are only meaningful if the behavior is not duplicated in the future.

This entire process involves not only the willingness to take ownership of our mistakes, but to forgive ourselves as well. Forgiveness is a healing balm. Many things in our life weigh heavy upon our hearts and consciousness, especially when we know that we have done wrong. A cloud of disappointment often hangs over us along with the sheer knowledge that we screwed up at something or in some situation. It is especially painful if we have hurt others through our actions. We often expend our energy and dampen our own spirit by psychologically beating ourselves up. My favorite female country singer, Reba McEntire, provides this encouraging advice in her song "*Walk On,*"

"Don't just stand there in the storm,
Walk towards the light til you find the sun
And you'll be better off in the long run. Walk on!"

Our feelings of remorse and regret are quite normal. They signify that we have a healthy moral compass that is working properly and seeks to keep us on course in life. Part of our process in managing our mistakes is to understand where they have their origin. If our actions, words and behavior are out of good intention and simply come up short, that is one thing. However, if we act out of anger, fear or a desire to act in a revengeful manner and something goes awry, then that is quite a different and disturbing story. Acts of revenge do not serve to make the wrong right. The usual outcome is to expand the hurt and anger for all involved and even other innocent parties that might become collateral damage. Each day is priceless and irreplaceable. Do we really want to spend our time dwelling on anger and hurt? The longer we allow regret and depression over past mistakes to drag us down, the less time we have to truly create and experience a joyful life.

Our lives are thrown into crisis mode many times in a single day. We move in and out of small doses of both success and failures as we move through daily existence. Trying and failing is not a disgrace. The only people who never fail or make mistakes are those who never put themselves out there on the limbs that expose us to our weaknesses and our critics. One of life's ironies is that the more successful we become, often the more critics we accrue. It is also in these precise situations from which we draw our strength and our will to succeed…to be better. It is not our mistakes in life that define us but rather how we deal with them and overcome them to make ourselves stronger. Show me a person's attitudes and reactions to their mistakes and errors in life and I can provide you with a vivid portrait of their strength and their character. Author Oscar Wilde tells us that, *"Experience is simply the name that we give to our mistakes."*

Now that I have touched on the easy part--our mistakes--it's time to delve into the mystical and life altering topic of forgiveness. Our mistakes are ours to own. Forgiving ourselves is a major chore, but the hardest forgiveness is that which we offer to others. The great Mahatma Gandhi shared, *"The weak can never forgive. Forgiveness is the attribute of the strong."* Of all our emotional, psychological and human actions, forgiveness is the most difficult to offer up to others. To understand the power of forgiveness is to understand the power that your anger and hurt has in holding you captive to the past. Once the genie is out of the bottle and you have been hurt or wronged, it can never be undone, but it can be forgiven. Holding anger and hate inside is a poison. We hold the notion that through anger and hate we can punish someone. It is only later that we discover that the damage done is usually within our own mind and approach to life and other people.

Forgiving someone does not mean you have excused their behavior. I can't control the emotions, actions and deeds of others. What I can control is my attitude to release and let go of the emotional damage and baggage that may be associated with the wrongs perpetrated against me. I can essentially, through forgiveness, put the ball of emotional clutter into the hands of the other person and rid myself of the burden. I can free my mind, heart and spirit to move forward and release the shackles that bind me to carrying anger and ill feelings through my life. I cannot give my positive energy and love to myself and the world if I am obsessed with anger and resentment for someone else.

In the Bible, Jesus urges us to forgive those who sin against us as many times as necessary. He also offered the profound and ultimate forgiveness to those who persecuted and crucified him. I will share this quote from an unknown source, *"Forgiveness is unlocking the door to set someone free and realizing that you were the prisoner."* Your heart can only be full of love if it has been filled by forgiveness and compassion. The peace that we experience in life is the peace and we generate for ourselves. President Abraham Lincoln shared that, *"People are as happy as they make up their minds to be."* Joy and peace are a state of mind…so is hate and depression. The choice is ours to make every day.

We have often heard the phrase, *"forgive and forget."* Personally, I'm not quite sure which one of these actions is the easiest to perform. Human nature and our sense of self-preservation dictates that we will most likely not *"forget"* the wrongs and harms that have come our way or the sources of that pain. In fact, I tend to embrace that the lessons learned from the train wrecks of our past are significant learning opportunities and guides for our future. The important message in the *"forget"* part of that instruction is that we don't hang onto the hurt or animosity after we have chosen to forgive. We don't reach into our bag of emotional and psychological weapons in the future to beat someone over the head with behaviors and situations that we have offered forgiveness for in the past. To continue to hang this metaphorical axe over someone's head indefinitely means that we have not truly forgiven nor have we released the associated anger and pain. I think a more appropriate phrase for my own life would be to *"forgive and release."* I also believe that we create our own *"karma"* in life. I do not seek to hold grudges or keep score when I trust that the perfect and right lessons are presented to each of us in our life…even those who have injured us in some manner.

Forgiveness is a general term but the process of us truly granting forgiveness should have some basic identifiable components. First, we should realize that those who we wish to forgive may be oblivious to the fact that they have hurt us in some manner. Often, those that we seek to forgive may have even transitioned into their next spiritual journey. Forgiveness comes more from the personal pivot in our thoughts and consciousness about the person and or event for which we seek to forgive. I don't have to have a face to face sit down with someone to forgive and release their actions in my own mind and heart. The manner in which we process our forgiveness is individual and personal.

I will offer my own road map to forgiveness that has served me well through the years as I have wrestled with letting go of anger, frustrations and discontent. Step one is to clearly identify what action or behavior you are forgiving in yourself or in others. You may write this down as an exorcism of such, or simply wish to hold it in your present thoughts. Next, I just affirm to myself and the universe that I forgive and release any negative energy, thoughts or feelings surrounding the event and or person. Finally, I bless the person who is the object of my forgiveness and free the space in my consciousness for positive and future interactions with this person and all others. Author William Paul Young in his bestselling book *The Shack* offered these words,

> *"Forgiveness is not about forgetting. It is about letting go of another person's throat... Forgiveness does not create a relationship...Forgiveness in no way requires that you trust the one you forgive...Forgiveness does not excuse anything."*

At its onset, the forgiving process may require us to repeat the thoughts and words of this ritual several hundred times a day each day until a new freedom of love and consciousness replaces the spaces once filled with anger and hate. It is through the repetition of our forgiving thoughts that we will grow comfortable and accepting of our actions. Always keep in the forefront that it is our own freedom that we seek. Forgiveness should be unconditional. To attach strings to our forgiveness is to remain bound to the conditions we seek to forgive. Forgiveness is not the same as reconciliation for at times we may offer our forgiveness but not choose to renew or continue a relationship if one had existed before. Reconciliation, if chosen, most likely should come with some guarantees and conditions that are honest, sincere and acceptable to all parties.

In his book *The Five People You Meet in Heaven*, Mitch Albom provides this insight, *"In order to move on, you must understand why you felt what you did and why you no longer need to feel it."* The significant principle to remember is that time and life marches on. We can never go back or retrieve even one single moment of the past. Our destiny, our joy, our peace of mind depends on how we use our experiences, good and bad to craft a happy and loving future for ourselves. We all will make mistakes and we all will hope for forgiveness at some point in our lives. If I am not willing to give forgiveness, how then can I expect to be forgiven when I yearn for it? To err is to exhibit our essential humanness. To grant forgiveness is to show the depth of our love for ourselves and for humanity. It requires strength of character and humility to say *"I'm sorry"* and ask for forgiveness. It takes love and a desire to push the world one small step closer to unity and healing to forgive.

Lesson Fifteen

Teammates in Life- I Am My Brother's Keeper

> *"The two strongest and longest relationships that you will ever have are the one with God and the one with yourself. They deserve a high degree of your time and attention."*
>
> **Fred Clausen**

Each of our lives are built on one distinct and dynamic underlying theme; our relationships. No one can navigate the tricky currents of existence without the help, motivation, encouragement and support of others. From the time we are born until the time we make our transition back into the infinite energy of the universe, we are buoyed by the symbiotic relationships that we nurture and embrace. Those who proclaim they can make it through life alone are crafting themselves a destiny to live a lonely life. I open my eyes, my mind and my heart to the understanding that I am related to every person and everything in God's universe. It is my charge and yours as well, to develop those relationships that provide a mutually beneficial opportunity to everyone for love, peace, happiness and understanding.

I deeply believe that I have a duty to the sacred brotherhood of man to work towards finding a mutual respect and acceptance of all people. I need to listen with empathy and communicate with clarity to gain a greater understanding of the reality of walking in another person's shoes. As singer Phil Collins suggested in song, for me personally, today is simply, *"Another Day in Paradise."* Acknowledging that, what then can I do for others who may be walking through their own personal hell today? My personal dedication to peace, love and understanding is very eloquently spelled out in the lyrics of the chorus from Celine Dion's song, *"Because You Loved Me."*

> *"You were my strength when I was weak*
> *You were my voice when I couldn't speak*
> *You were my eyes when I couldn't see*
> *You saw the best there was in me*
> *Lifted me up when I couldn't reach*
> *You gave me faith 'cause you believed*
> *I'm everything I am*
> *Because you loved me"*

I want my legacy to be as the person referenced in this song that is the strength for the weak, the voice for the voiceless and the eyes for the blind. I want to be that champion of a person who looks for and encourages the best in everyone. I want to live in such a manner that the words from Matthew 25:40 in the Bible describe me as one who served God and man by doing even the smallest of the things in life. I sincerely believe that by serving man, I serve and honor God as well. I accept the role to serve as my brother's keeper in an effort to bring a richer and fuller life for all.

My athletic adventures have had a profound and lasting impact on my ability to establish, maintain and grow relationships of every kind. The characteristic of forming lasting bonds with teammates provides the blue print necessary to forge those same productive and meaningful relationships in the other areas of our lives. If you aren't a good teammate, how can you expect to be good in a committed relationship that requires all the same qualities? In a strange, but meaningful sense, all our relationships have roots in our own self-interest. That is not to assume that we embrace a selfish attitude, but rather that the natural mutualism of any relationship requires us to look at both the benefit, that we can provide as well as the benefits that we can derive.

Life is by nature a team sport and meant to be engaged in and enjoyed to the fullest with our family, friends and the rest of mankind. When I speak of relationships, I am inclusive of any and all contact and impact that we have as we stroll through our lives. I want to acknowledge the role of our human relationships, but also of those with nature, the environment, ourselves and with God and the universe. I want my life's light to shine upon the relationships with those close to me and also with those whom I may never come into contact but with whom I share a universal consciousness and awareness. I exude a hunger to develop a deeper and more meaningful understanding of why and how our lives are intertwined with every atom of matter, every spark of energy and every conscious thought that has ever existed.

Songs and movies abound about relationships born out of the magnetic human attraction and romantic love. Many others lift the veil on deeper, more profound matters of the heart, mind and soul. There are so many in fact that we are often numbed to the overwhelming evidence that it is indeed the web-like entanglement of all our relationships that give lasting substance to who we are, what we believe and where we focus our energy. I dare say that we are a divine and beautiful product of all the relationships that we experience in our life.

The nucleus of the swirling energy and information in our existence has its core in first and foremost, the relationship that we forge with ourselves. I can't love others and all of God's creations if I do not first revere the beauty and love that exists in me and as me. When is the last time you looked into a mirror and told yourself something that sounded vaguely like this? *"You is Kind. You is Smart. You is Important."* How do those famous words from the movie *The Help* resonate in your life? Actress Viola Davis' character in the movie, Aibileen Clark, used those words to help guide a young and impressionable little girl through her first lesson about her true and beautiful self-worth. Do we not owe ourselves the same kindness and love that we seek to give to others? The two strongest and longest relationships that you will ever have are the one with God and the one with yourself. They deserve a high degree of your time and attention.

So, let's stroll through life together a bit and examine some of the many types of relationships that will have a profound impact on our lives. I have already mentioned the relationship with ourselves in introspection of who we are and why we are here. Closely following that inner awareness is our relationships with our partners, family, friends, colleagues, the world in general and mankind in particular. Of course, then there is our spiritual connection that unites us with the infinite power and wisdom of God, whatever you perceive that to be. A true relationship with a Supreme Being or power requires us to acknowledge the presence and energy that connects us to the entity.

The God that I know, and embrace may not have the same name in reference as yours, but the universal power that funnels to the same omnipotent energy is the same. There are many paths to a relationship to the one God. I choose to believe that any road that leads to the same destination of peace, love and understanding is a divine and blessed route. I pray to speak to God and then I meditate in quiet solitude to listen to God's reply. Our spiritual practices to hone our personal relationship with God and the universe are as individual and diverse as our own finger prints and personality. As my Father used to tell me, *"I can't worry about someone else's business when I have my own fish to fry."*

Any of our meaningful relationships must be solidly grounded in several key and non-negotiable shared characteristics. I personally consider the essential foundational cornerstones of building a relationship to be honesty, trust, respect and communication. Once we have an established relationship, then the daily maintenance plan for growing and nurturing it includes what I have come to know as the four A's of relationships: Acceptance, Appreciation, Attention and Affection. Much like a garden of beautiful and fragrant flowers and delicate plants, we must constantly tend to our relationships to ensure that they will survive, grow and thrive. Every relationship we spawn, like every flower and every snowflake, will have a distinctive pattern and life that is unique unto itself. No two relationships will mirror each other as the dynamics and personalities that are engaged are exclusive to the parties involved and to the place and time.

A relationship is how we interact with others and the foundations upon which those interactions are based. My relationship with my wife is different than those with my sons and daughter, which in turn are different than those with my friends, which in turn are different than those with work and business colleagues. All of these relationships require honesty, trust, respect and communication but the more personal the relationship the more we move into a deeper heartfelt and emotion driven awareness and approach. Much like an Olympic diver is scored on their degree of difficulty, there is greater difficulty to sustaining a long and loving relationship with partners and family. There is also a greater reward when executing the more difficult related tasks over the course of a lifetime.

    I will offer also that even our closest, most personal relationships sometimes change from one degree to another. Some of my friends and family marvel at the relationships that I maintain with the four women who have been my marriage partners along my life's journey. Obviously, my best advice is to not have so many to start with. I have, however, had the understanding that a person who I loved deeply once is still someone who I love and have concern and compassion for, even if the parameters and dynamics of the relationship have changed. The romantic love has evaporated into a more profound love of someone who I once shared landmark life moments, children, trials and tribulations. They were my confidants and teammates. I stand witness to the fact that through love, communication and a desire to understand each other, former partners can still stand steadfast in their support and respect for each other. They can remain an essentially important person in one's life.

    I have sought to find kindness rather than bitterness. I have been the cause of distress and have been the recipient of the same. Jesus set the tone for me when he instructed, *"Let he who is without sin cast the first stone."* I have asked for forgiveness and given it as well. I have chosen to love and support rather than condemn and isolate. I have chosen to enter a different type of relationship on a different plane in life, but one which still is kind and supportive. So much of what others may view as odd, like having my wife and two former wives together for a family holiday event or birthday, I choose to see as an extended family gathering. Am I not responsible for showing my children and grandchildren what forgiveness and love look like in action? What others declare is the impossible in after-marriage relationships, I see as a masterful new relationship model based upon a new honesty, trust, respect and communication after the marriage ended.

Sometimes in sports as in life, we must support and lift up our teammates, even when they have stumbled and put the game at risk. It is no different in our life challenges. We must love and honor the imperfection of humanity as well as the imperfection in ourselves. As a husband, wife, parent, teacher, friend, mentor or coach, it is our challenge to cultivate the relationship that feeds on honesty, trust, respect and loving communication rather than shame, humiliation and fear. When we deal with colleagues, business associates or even the checker at the grocery store, our best strategy is to work to establish the fundamental notion that each person in the relationship is important, valued and whose input and ideas are worth consideration. Everyone wants to be made to feel special. Everyone yearns to be respected. The judgment of your true ability to forge solid relationships lies in how you treat those in your life from whom you have nothing to gain. Anyone can put forward a supportive façade for personal gain. The measure of your authenticity lies in your consistent interactions and dealings with all people.

I may have hinted to you that the four A's of relationships might only be reserved for romantic relationships. Not so! We all want to feel the warmth of acceptance. It is a lack of acceptance that has caused the world to stumble for ages as man has sought to *"change"* others rather than embracing and accepting differences. We have far more in common than we have differences. One of the greatest of all feelings is the warmth and joy of being appreciated. Life and our tasks can be hard at times. As in sports, we are often asked to go above and beyond what the normal expectations would be. Going that extra mile, covering that extra shift for a friend, helping someone move, or simply opening a door for a stranger can become a daily blessing for us if the kind words of appreciation are floated back our way. There is such tremendous power in a sincere and heartfelt *"thank you."*

Acceptance and appreciation spark a feeling of peace and serenity in our mind, heart and in our souls which brings the joy in life bubbling to the surface. It is through these expressions that we feel the attention of another connected being which is aimed directly at us and for the purpose of lifting us up in some manner. We all love attention and recognition. We all feed on the excitement that washes over us when we have the undivided attention of someone who we love and respect. It is a gift that can only be matched by the affection that is afforded to us as an accent on the relationships in our lives.

Affection comes to us in a variety of ways. Sometimes we are embraced with a hug. Other times we might be the recipient of a kiss, or quite possibly both a hug and kiss in a choreographed display of love and respect, which solidifies and reassures us that we are special and worthy in the eyes of the giver. Sometimes affection comes our way with a simple pat on the back, or from someone holding our hand as we walk quietly together. The heart, mind, body and soul thrive on affection. Sometimes affection is administered as part of a simple gesture of words, cards, flowers or gifts directed to encompass the entire arsenal of acceptance, appreciation, attention and affection.

Our personal world balances on our human interactions and relationships with others. Some of these relationships last a lifetime. Some we move into and out of with time. Some are situational, and others are just in our lives by chance. Aside from these human interactions, there are other vitally important relationships that have a profound effect on our life as well. We are spiritual beings on a human journey. We are one with God and one with the universe. We have an inherent relationship with nature and the environment along with an obligation to provide the same acceptance, appreciation, attention and affection to that part of our world. We are the conscious creators of our own physical world--of our own environment. We are also the guardians of nature and its infinite beauty and amazing creatures.

Ralph Waldo Emerson shared profoundly with us, *"The Earth laughs in flowers."* Then does it also paint with sunlight and shed tears as raindrops? Einstein proclaimed that, *"The environment is everything that isn't me."* This all-encompassing relationship with the planet is one we simply cannot afford to ignore. Like all other relationships, we must play an active role in nurturing the care and protection of our planet. We cannot hope that someone else in some future generation will step forward in our stead. The great and wise Indian Chief Seattle reminded us with the reflection, *"We do not inherit the earth from our ancestors; we borrow it from our children."* The relationship between man and the environment in the present will determine how future generations will be able to embrace God's beauty and magnificence. We are the keepers of both our brothers and our world. We cannot and must not turn a blind eye or shirk that responsibility out of indifference or for the selfishness of perceived financial or political gain. If it is to be, it is up to me.

I have been witness to the best in man and also the worst in man. We are the architects of our past, present and future and the relationships that we forge. The grandest of all connections will rest in our personal relationship between ourselves and the omnipresent power of God and our universe. To know God is to know ourselves. To discover the divine center of our mind and soul is to acknowledge the same God spark of energy in all people. The hunger within us to find our purpose is a gnawing desire to reveal the God energy within our being. Across the world there are many names for God, many perceptions of God and many teachings about God. There is no right God and wrong God when the origin is in love. The one constant is that whether consciously and openly or within the secret shadows of our mind, we all harbor an inquisitive nature and an innate desire to have a relationship with God. We yearn to connect to the divine energy that permeates everything. It is this relationship that will be infinitely our most important and profound.

Lesson Sixteen

The Game's Not Over Until You Complete Your Bucket List

> *"To squander the moments and sit idly by will produce a dull, uneventful and unrewarding highlight reel of our time on the planet. It is not enough for us simply to make a bucket list...we must seek to live it."*
>
> Fred Clausen

I had the opportunity to watch the movie *The Bucket List* again a few days ago. I often watch movies that I like over and over again in an effort to catch phrases, thoughts and nuances that I may not have picked up on the first time. I am sure most of us do the same thing from time to time. In my efforts to pull this collection of essays together and have closure, I will draw a bit more from the philosophy of Yogi Berra and some of the most poignant lessons from *The Bucket List*. I will also seek to weave the lessons of the collection into my summation. Wow, who would think that two great, but crusty, character actors like Morgan Freeman and Jack Nicholson could bring tears to my eyes while Yogi quotes bring me tears of laughter? I still have so much to learn and so much life yet to live and service to give. We all do!

My first great Yogism in this summation is the profound statement that *"If the world were perfect, then it wouldn't be."* I know--you just laughed out loud. So did I--for the one hundredth time. However, digging deeper into these quips I center on the possible meaning that if we truly lived in a perfect world, then there would be no need for us to ever work towards and accomplish anything. There would be no need to think, to dream, to create, to love, to help, to show compassion if all were already perfect in our world. Precisely what is our mental picture of a perfect world? If it is not perfect already, then what are we doing each day to bring it closer to that perfection? I contend that if we don't experience some of the imperfect and uncomfortable times in life how are we supposed to recognize the good and the perfect? It is our own creative energy and efforts that will bring the planet closer to perfection.

So many things in our lives are about each of us individually, yet so much more swirls around the dynamics of our thoughts, interactions, and relationships with others. We are hungry for independence and self reliance yet can only feel complete, useful and appreciated when in the service of others. Those who live to serve only themselves then serve no one. The American singer, songwriter and author Gerald Way shared, *"Being happy doesn't mean that everything is perfect. It means you have decided to look beyond the imperfections."* We must become agents of change and change that is manifested in making the world a more joyful and a better place for all. Jack Nicholson's character in *The Bucket List* shared another profound quote from Gerald Way, *"One day your life will flash before your eyes. Make sure it's worth watching."* To squander the moments and sit idly by will produce a dull, uneventful and unrewarding highlight reel of our time on the planet. It is not enough for us simply to make a bucket list…we must seek to live it.

Our world is imperfect, but it should be our quest to awaken our spiritual nature to be in tuned to God and the universe and move it closer in that direction. Finding that seed within ourselves and conducting our life with a universal awareness and impeccable integrity, gives us an opportunity to become a difference maker. We then can bring our world a little closer to a more perfect peace and understanding. We need to engage and be hands on in our efforts and recognize that the world is a diverse and beautiful place. We must offer respect to the majesty of Mother Nature as well as to the many shades of skin tones, languages and concepts of God. We must keep our minds open and our hearts open even wider to the changing dynamics that drive our lives or suffer being left behind and without an educated voice. To honor others in our world brings honor to our own life. To honor diversity brings dignity to all men. To offer unconditional love and compassion is to honor whatever your concept is of an omnipresent God and divine energy in the universe.

The impact of our actions is determined by our willingness to have a big picture mentality that drives us towards universal love and understanding. Staying in the dense fog of ignorance will only diminish our ability to see and experience the truth of life and hamper our efforts at becoming an effective agent for change. Change will happen and is inevitable with or without us. Let our own love and acceptance be that change that we seek to see in the world. Ralph Waldo Emerson shared these words, *"What lies behind you and what lies in front of you, pales in comparison to what lies inside you."* Call your own plays in life. Be the captain of your ship and the master of your soul.

Become keenly aware of the importance of time and timing and be able to make concrete decisions based upon your knowledge and experience. Precious moments and times in our lives are only available in the here and now. We can't be afraid to call the play, or we will possibly forfeit the opportunity to become a difference maker in our life and in the lives of others. We can't allow fear to paralyze our efforts to bring our life out of the shadows and into the light so that we might shine in our existence. Taking calculated risks based on valid information and instinctive hypothesis is what has advanced our world and mankind over the millenniums. The fear that often impales us is only a mirage sent to distract us and cast a shadow over the sight and resolve to reach our goals. The world needs and deserves the best version of ourselves. Focus on the important things in life rather than the smoke and mirror antics of the *"me only"* entourage.

What items are inscribed on your personal bucket list of things you want to see, do and accomplish with your time here on earth? The ancient Egyptian proverb shared by Morgan Freeman's character in *The Bucket List* revealed the two-pointed questions that we all must answer at life's transition; *"Have you found joy in your life? Has your life brought joy to others?"* This simplistic evaluation invites us to examine what we have done for ourselves through our experiences. More importantly, what have we sought to do for others? This measuring stick of existence reassures us that it is not where we start in our life, but how we progress and what we accomplish along the way that makes the journey worthwhile. It is our awareness to attend not only our own needs, but those of our family, friends and even the strangers who fate brings across our path. In life's review it is never *"one and done,"* but rather an audit of the total body of our work here on the planet.

Playing in the game of life requires much of us. We must be disciplined. We must be courageous and bold. We must be honest and compassionate. We must use our time prudently and constructively. We must care for our body and our health while also guarding the health and well being of mankind and the environment. We must be willing to put others ahead of ourselves at times as a gesture of love and kindness. We must work to create and enjoy the prosperity of life in our personal finances, our health, our relationships and our achievements. We must get off the bench and become one of life's impact players on many levels. We must develop our God given talents and seek to discover others with our thoughts and consciousness. Through prayer and meditation, we must learn to take our spiritual being to the quiet place of the most high as we seek direction and affirmation. The great Sir William Wallace, medieval leader of the Scottish people stated, *"Every man dies, not every man really lives."* We are given the gift of life. What we do with it is up to us.

President Abraham Lincoln once told us, *"In the end, it's not the years in your life that count. It's the life in your years."* Lincoln was a wise man who recognized that the best of living is not in the quantity but rather in the quality of our life. We don't have to be wealthy or famous to have a great life. We can have joy and satisfaction in life without having to push, shove and bully our way to being first in line for everything. The universe has an abundant supply for all our needs and desires. The Bible tells us in Matthew 7:7, *"Ask and it shall be given to you; seek and you will find; knock and the door will be opened to you."* Our thoughts and prayers will manifest our earthly reality.

The single most important dynamic in our life is the *"how"* element. When a magician dazzles the audience, we all seek to learn how the trick was performed. The magic in assessing our life is in *"how you play the game."* It is the *"how"* that will make us memorable; How did I live? How did I love? How did I treat others? How did I share? How did I reach out and display compassion, honesty and integrity? How did I make a difference and how was I a blessing to others? If we cannot pass the test of the *"how"* questions, the rest is irrelevant. Life requires that we be graded on the performance indicators of universal love, service and significance.

Each day we have the choice to be happy, positive and a blessing to ourselves and others. Many things in our life we cannot control, but we are the one who controls our attitude, our thoughts and our actions. I have accountability to myself, God and the universe. I implore each of us to exhibit a builder not a wrecker mentality. It takes no skill in life to tear things and people down. A sharp tongue and destructive behavior can tear apart what others have taken years to build up, both physically and psychologically. I encourage you to take the talents that you have been endowed with and use them to build a life of love and admiration for all of God's creations.

Our existence will not be error free. Each of us will have to work constantly to minimize our mistakes, control our emotions and temper and master our words. Conscious awareness of our actions and their impact on others is a requirement, not an elective in life. We all walk through life vulnerable to hurt and distress each day. We teeter upon the behavior and our own words that can cause pain to others as well. Through careless thoughts and deeds mankind self inflicts needless hurt, unrest and resentment. It is up to us to change that dynamic. Above all of this fray we must strive to live an engaged life that offers apologetic refrains when needed and warranted. We must also dispense the healing and soul freeing compassion of forgiveness.

My parting thought takes me to 2 Timothy 4:7, *"I have fought the good fight, I have finished the race, I have kept the faith."* I have been blessed in many ways. You too can start today in the present moment and make that adventurous journey as well. As Yogi would say, *"It ain't over til it's over,"* so make the moments matter. Morgan Freeman summed it up in *The Bucket List* with *"We live, we die, and the wheels on the bus go round and round."* Time and our life opportunities are truly evaporating rapidly into the future. Don't waste another day, hour or minute. Find your passion, share your love and remember, *"It's how you play the game"* that will define your legacy, your memories and your happiness. In the end, any path that we have chosen from the fork in the road can lead us home.

Parting Poem

If I Could

If I could give you one special gift
To hold and enhance your life,
I'd give you the warmth of endless love
And freedom from all of life's strife.

If I could grant you one special wish
To fill and brighten your years,
I'd grant that you age gently and kind
And that your eyes shed very few tears.

If I could leave you one special impression
To wander among your dreams,
I'd leave you the image of your own warm smile
And the taste of your favorite ice cream.

If I could take you to one special place
To guide and comfort your soul,
I'd take you so gently to heaven's door
And regret not for being so bold.

If I could hear your laughter erupt
To again fill a room full of cheer,
I'd hear treasured moments shared by us all
And feel lucky for having you near.

If I could impart to you one last thought
To remember my time with you here,
I'd impart that my soul has been totally blessed
And your life has made it so dear.

By Fred Clausen
December 2013

About the Author

Fred Clausen is an educator, author and motivational speaker who has spent over forty years in public education. He enjoyed a successful career as a teacher, coach and athletic administrator. Fred is a Past-President of the Texas High School Athletic Directors Association (THSADA), after having served as President in 2007-08. He was honored as the High School *"Athletic Director of the Year"* for the state of Texas in 2008 and selected for induction into the Texas High School Athletic Directors *"Hall of Honor"* in 2009. Fred currently serves as the District Director of Athletic Programs for the Dallas County Community College District and the Dallas Metro Athletic Conference Commissioner.

Fred has also served for six years on the Board of Directors of Unity Church of Dallas, most recently as the Board President 2016-18. Unity of Dallas is a new thought ministry that embraces positive, practical Christianity that is free of judgment and full of love. His relationship with Unity began in 1987. Fred's life experiences have led him on a variety of spiritual quest, but the Unity core messages of unconditional love and prosperity consciousness have always drawn him back. His solid spiritual foundation is now permanently settled in Unity where the love, acceptance, and a mindset of both prosperity and abundance provide daily inspiration and motivation on his human journey.

Fred is also the author of the book **"The Essential Elements of Successful Coaching"**. His book has been used in many coaching seminars, professional growth programs and college classrooms as a valuable aide to educating both young coaches and veterans alike.

www.ingramcontent.com/pod-product-compliance
Lightning Source LLC
LaVergne TN
LVHW051118080426
835510LV00018B/2113